WILD SIDE

A Novel

James Bell

James Bell

Also by James Bell

The Screen Door: A Story of Love, Letters and Travel

The Twenty-Year Chafe

Christchurch

Crisis in the Congo

American Dreamer

Spook

Condor

James Bell

This is a work of historical fiction. Certain names, characters, places and incidents are the product of the author's imagination or are used fictitiously.

Copyright © 2024 James Bell
All rights reserved.

Library of Congress Registration Number: TXu 2-424-019

Bell, James
Wild Side: a novel
Historical Fiction

ISBN: 9798832177083
Printed in the United States of America

Dedication

To Heidi, my muse, best friend, and wife of 38 years, and to my daughters, Virginia and Eliza.

James Bell

'London is satisfied, Paris is resigned, but New York is always hopeful. Always it believes that something good is about to come off, and it must hurry to meet it.'

Dorothy Parker, New Yorker Magazine, *1928*

'I happen to like New York, I happen to love this town
I like the city air, I like to drink of it
The more I see New York, the more I think of it
I like the sight and the sound and even the stink of it
I happen to like New York.'

Bobby Short, Café Carlyle, 1974

'If I played in New York, they'd name a candy bar after me.'

Reggie Jackson, New York Yankees, 1977-1981

James Bell

One

Spring 2000

She hadn't planned on a solitary life, but Angie deGraaf had come to relish it. She read voraciously, ate sparingly, and rarely entertained visitors. When she ventured out – to return a library book. or collect her mail – she greeted postal clerks, neighbors, and cashiers alike by name, asking after the baby, the puppy, or the college-bound son.

A silver-streaked strawberry blonde, tall and long-limbed, Angie favored fleece vests and hiking shoes like everyone else in Stowe. She wore her hair twisted into a loose bun, securing it with a tortoise clamp or, in a pinch, a chopstick. No one suspected that this fifty-something woman was once famous. But that was about to change.

Angie loved springtime in Vermont. Once the skis were stored, mud season would last well into May. From her deck, a light breeze set the new leaves clattering, as the mountains in the distance softened and greened. Above her, red robins flanked the orderly armies of Canada geese returning to New England's golf courses. And from the valley, the percussion of nail guns signaled the human woodpeckers were back too, building new houses, which were now called timeshares.

May Zhang had never met Angie. But as May researched her story, she had to admit, she'd developed a girl-crush. It was time to give her a call. From her desk in New York, May practiced her opening line, took a breath, and dialed.

Angie stood at her kitchen sink, washing a week's worth of coffee cups, when her cordless phone rang. She turned off the faucet, dried her hands on a dish towel, and stepped onto the deck, phone in hand.

May introduced herself. She was calling from *Rolling Stone* magazine. She introduced herself as a staff writer. Angie couldn't fathom why such a person would be calling her. "The magazine is planning a throwback series on 'Sounds of the '70s,' May explained. Her voice sounded young, polite, and a little breathless. "I'd like to write a profile for the section, tell your story," she added.

Rolling Stone? My story? Angie sat down to take in this information. She felt flattered that anyone would include her on such a list. And *Rolling Stone*, no less. Still, the prospect of talking to a reporter stirred up feelings of dread.

"Would it be possible for us to meet?" May asked in her cheerful upspeak. "The 25th anniversary of your hit single is coming up — as I'm sure you know. The date coincides nicely with our issue. If you're up for that, I'd like to do an interview."

She did not know, nor had she given a moment's thought to her song's anniversary. How did *Rolling Stone* know? Or better, why would they care? What else did they know? She felt flattered, of course, that anyone would include her song on such a list, much less *Rolling Stone*.

"Would next Friday work for *you*?" May asked. "I could drive up from the city and stay in town for the weekend."

Angie hesitated. Her disco hit, 'Deep, Deep, Deep' soared to number one on the 1975 Billboard charts. When a reporter from the *New York Times* called, she agreed to an interview, cautioning that not *all* her news was fit to print. The reporter assured her she was more interested in her meteoric rise, playing the fangirl to gain her trust. When the *Times* published a salacious hit piece three weeks later, the betrayal stung. She hadn't given an interview since then.

"Mrs. *deGraaf*?" May asked. "Did we lose our connection? I missed what you said …"

Angie had said nothing. She didn't know *what* to say. "Let me check my calendar," she answered, turning the blank pages, buying time. The girl sounded so sincere. She didn't have the heart to turn her down. But before she could say yes, she made a mental note to invite Clara up for the weekend, to keep her inside the guardrails.

Like Angie, Clara left Idaho alone to escape their LDS family. She'd turned up in New York, at Angie's apartment door to be precise, sixteen years ago. Angie welcomed her, offering her the couch, where Clara slept for a couple of weeks before finding three nice-enough roommates seeking a fourth. Clara found a job in a Chelsea flower market. But she was never a city girl. She moved Manchester within a year, taking a job as a ranger for the U.S. Forestry Service.

"That would be fine," Angie told May, speaking carefully. May thanked her profusely, audibly relieved. "I've been doing some research on Studio 54; the whole era is fascinating! I can't wait to meet you – and hear more," she added. They exchanged a few logistical details before wrapping up the call. May thanked her again. And again. Then wished Angie a "great day," and said goodbye.

Angie clicked the phone off and set it down. Then she fixed her gaze at the mountains to steady herself. Still a soft touch, she still struggled to say no. She'd call Clara that evening to make sure she could come. As she jotted her note-to-self, a Cole Porter lyric popped into her head: *Po-tay-to po-tah-to; to-may-to to-mah-to ... Let's call the whole thing off!*

Two

Stowe gets eight times more snow than Lewiston, Idaho in the winter, according to the U.S. Weather Service. It smells better, too. The pulp and paper factories in Angie's hometown send a steady plume of white smoke into the air. Like Lewiston itself, the smell, a mix of wet dog and charred wood, was impossible to escape. The olfactory lobes of the locals adapted, normalizing the offensive odor, until they hardly noticed it.

Unless they worked for the paper mill, nobody moved to Lewiston on purpose. Angie was proud to note the town's star exception, an unknown rookie ball player named Reggie Jackson, who played 12 games for Lewiston's minor league team, the Broncs, in the summer of 1966.

Angie was a teenager then, watching from the packed bleachers with friends on a summer night when Reggie stepped up to the plate.

When the pitcher released his fastball, he swung with the full force of his body, propelling the ball like a meteor with pure, sweet power. It sailed quickly, high over the diamond, beyond the left field fence, and through her uncle's kitchen window. The ball rolled across the linoleum over the glass shards, coming to rest only at the refrigerator.

After sweeping up the glass and replacing the broken pane, her uncle presented the ball to Angie, given that she witnessed Jackson's home run. Jackson was called up to Modesto soon after and, by the following season, he'd made it to the Majors. He'd go on to hit 567 career homers, but the Hall of Famer never forgot that first one, or that summer night in Lewiston, Idaho.

Angie checked her watch. The reporter was due in a few hours. She'd made up the guestroom for Clara, but still had some cleaning to do. She opened the living room windows to catch the afternoon breeze, then she stood back, arms crossed, to survey the bookshelves through the critical eye of a visitor. The yellow spines of *National Geographic* magazines, lined up by the yard, were interspersed with *Readers Digest* condensed books, a Bertie Wooster collection, and painted duck decoys.

On the middle shelf, a quilted Chinese coolie hat, complete with a braid, had sat next to a Papuan penis gourd since at least the early sixties. She adjusted the framed photographs: Christian with Sly Stone, John Lindsay, and Bobby Short; his parents, Isaac and Marge with Duella, his childhood nanny turned lifelong family friend.

She opened a lower cabinet to search for two accordion files, one filled with airmail letters postmarked from faraway places. The other, a cache that Angie had exchanged with her grandmother, Ada. Organized by year, each letter remained in its original envelope. She set both files on the piano bench. They'd be handy for recalling dates or details. Clara would help with that, too.

Angie and Christian had decamped from New York's Upper West Side seventeen years ago, after he retired early from a brilliant career in advertising, once the corporate suits squeezed the last drop of joy from an industry that was once fun. By the '80s, New York had grown richer, while its residents grew angrier and less neighborly. In Vermont, they found the peace of the run-down family ski house sustained them. She would inherit the house years later, along with its pot-bellied stove, avocado green Kenmore refrigerator, and long list of repairs the deGraafs had put off until "someday."

She'd added the deck, replaced the fifty-year-old roof, and installed a dishwasher in the kitchen. New gutters and downspouts were next. When her in-laws built the A-frame in the 1930s, they'd fretted over every expense, despite their tony Upper East Side lineage. Now, Angie found, it was always something.

As she fluffed the living room cushions and dusted the piano, she thought, *you should get back to playing*. She'd been intending to reinvent herself. The singer-songwriter title sounded more dignified than former disco star. Maybe the *Rolling Stone* call was a nudge from the universe? If she didn't hop to it, she'd wind up with 'One-Hit-Wonder' carved on her headstone, her fleeting moment of fame dogging her into eternity.

Tires crunched on the gravel driveway. Angie peered through the open window, excited to see Clara's old green Saab bumping up the hill toward the house. Thank goodness. A throwback to Angie's era, Clara was an old soul and a tree hugger. *Rolling Stone* or not, she was fiercely protective of Angie. She parked at the house and burst from the car, barefoot, arms open for a hug. She wore a t-shirt and shorts, and she'd pulled her long hair through the back of a Red Sox cap and walked to the front door.

"You made good time," Angie said, folding Clara in her arms before standing back to take a look at her. She grabbed her duffle bag from the backseat of the Saab and walked toward the front door.

"Nobody on the road," Clara said with a shrug. "You know Vermont. It takes a good snowstorm to get everybody behind the wheel. When's your reporter coming? Aren't you *excited?*" Like her aunt, Clara was long limbed, with unruly strawberry blond hair. Clara broke into song as they entered the house, "*Rolling Stone … gonna see my picture on the cover …*"

"*… Gonna buy five copies for my mother,*" Angie continued, then rolled her eyes at the thought, as she pointed Clara inside. In the kitchen, Clara set her bag on the table and rummaged inside to produce the latest issue, with a brooding Sean Penn on the cover. "You've hit the big time auntie. Can I get your autograph?"

"Make me charming and I'll think about it," Angie said. "You look like you need a cold beer? Me too. Let's not stand on ceremony. The reporter's name is May; she's checking into the Village Inn first, so she'll get here a little after five. She sounds *very young*, but nice on the phone. It's supposed to be a nice weekend."

They stepped onto the deck and pulled two chairs side-by-side to face the mountains. "Cheers," Angie lifted her beer bottle and Clara reached for hers, to clink a toast. "I thought tonight called for a Mexican beer," Angie said wistfully. "Remember *El Sombrero?*"

"Never gonna forget that," she winked. They'd returned for Ada's funeral, navigating the awkward homecoming together, a pair of black sheep. Clara took a sip. For Angie, it had been seventeen years. By then, she'd blocked out much of her childhood. The visit stirred up a few fond memories, still, nothing had changed. The rift was final.

"What did the reporter say? What did she sound like?"

"She wants to know what New York was like in the 'sixties and 'seventies.' She told me she was born in 1974," Angie said, rolling her eyes "It's not just me. They're covering the hits of the era. But she called the article a 'Profile' so it sounds important," Angie paused. "I'm sure she'll ask about Idaho and the LDS church, Clara. She may be young, but the girl's done her homework. I still don't know if she's writing a gotcha piece or not. But I doubt it. Who'd bother anymore?" She smiled.

May pulled out of the CITGO station just south of Hanover, headed toward I-91. With just over two hours to go, she studied the Road Atlas on the passenger seat, then stepped on the gas pedal to merge onto the highway. She would check into the bed-and-breakfast first, then ring Mrs. deGraaf. "I've got all the time in the world," she'd told May. "My niece will be here. She's about your age. Hope that's okay. She can straighten my stories out."

May glanced at the speedometer and eased off of the pedal. The magazine wouldn't pay for a speeding ticket. Already, her editor was asking her to 'bring back a juicy story.' But that wasn't where her instincts – and her research – were leading. Angie's tale seemed to have the makings of a movie, or a love story. As she wound north along the Connecticut River, the mountains rose ahead. To shake off her worry, she fiddled with the radio, getting static, and more static, until she hit Lou Reed on the Dartmouth student station:

> … A hustle here and a hustle there
> New York City is the place where
> They said hey babe,
> Take a walk on the wild side
> I said hey Joe,
> Take a walk on the wild side
>
> And the colored girls say
> *Doo do doo do doo do doo do doo*
> *Doo do doo do doo do doo do doo*

Angela Love's song 'Deep, Deep, Deep' debuted in 1975, long before May's time. She'd listened to the album, dug up grainy footage of *The Angela Love Connection*; and watched as Angie danced on stage in a skimpy tasseled top, satin hot pants and white go-go boots, her big hair fortified by a can of Aqua Net hair spray.

The song's infectious beat brought the world to their feet and onto the dance floor, before beginning its steady climb up the charts. In the magazine's photo archives, May had found pictures of Angie dancing at Studio 54 with Yankee's player Reggie Jackson. By the time the disco was shuttered a few years later, Angie had married Christian and the song had hit number one.

She was getting close now. May noticed end-of-the-season ski sales, quaint bed and breakfasts, and ads for local realtors on the highway billboards. As she continued through the misty valley, mountains loomed large enough for May to make out its green ski trails. Angie had given her precise directions to the inn and, from there, to her 'chalet' as she called it, adding, "Come on by once you get settled."

Three

Angie greeted May warmly, ushering her onto the deck. "Thank you for having me," May said, surveying the view and spectacular orange sunset. "It's *beautiful* here." She declined Angie's offer of a beer in favor of a glass of lemonade. Then she set up her tape recorder, notebook, and pens on the large round table, along with a folder of news clippings.

As Angie settled back in her chair, May looked at both of them with a tentative smile. "So … let's get started. I've been wondering, what brought you to New York – and Vermont, in the first place?"

Angie looked to Clara, unsure where to begin. "A bus?" Clara suggested. This got them both laughing, but it failed to break the ice.

"Oh gosh, I'm so sorry," May said quickly. "I should have mentioned; this is just background. A conversation. We'll call it 'off-the-record' if you like. I'm just looking for the thread to establish the timeline. I don't have to put this in."

"Of course," Angie said, gathering her thoughts. "I'd never been further than Spokane Washington. I grew up in Idaho farm country. I'd never seen the ocean or set foot on a beach. The bus ride from Boise to New York opened my eyes to the wide-open country I'd thought existed only on TV or in the movies. Until I saw it for myself, none of it seemed real. But I'd given no thought to a career. In Idaho, you stayed put, got married and had babies. That was the path everyone took. So, I had no inkling of what I would do once I got to New York. Nana had given me some money to get going and I trusted I'd find work, eventually.

"After five days on the bus, we arrived at Penn Station. I searched the cab line for a driver who looked nice, then I slid into the backseat with my suitcase and read from the scrap of paper my grandmother had given me. 'The Barbizon Hotel, please. It's at 160 East Sixty-Third Street.' I'd practiced those words on the bus, so I sounded confident, like I knew what I was doing, at least.

"The taxi driver was heavy-set. He smiled at me in the rear-view mirror, saying, 'Yes, Miss.' He'd picked up a few girls like me, bound for the same address."

"I know it," he said. "That's a nice place for nice girls."

"I didn't go back for seventeen years. Thank God for Clara," she said, patting her niece's knee. "The place was like stepping into a time-warp, an isolated life in black and white."

"And the rift?" May asked. "What was that about? Is that what made you leave?"

Angie hesitated.

"*Why* are you *protecting* that asshole?" Clara said, bristling. "It's *your* story, Angie. *Own* it."

Jared Bingham fancied himself a ladies man, back in 1966. Eight years older, he'd been flirting with Angie for years, laying it on thick once she hit high school. The girls called him 'dreamy.' She enjoyed the attention and by 18, Angie was crushing hard. A virgin then; she saw it clearly now. LDS girls were easy prey.

"Come over Saturday," he whispered into the phone, stirring the butterflies in her stomach. "Game's on TV, kick off at seven. We'll watch it together."

"It was kissing until he grabbed at my blouse …" Angie began. It happened so fast. One minute he was gently caressing her back. The next, she was pinned to the sofa, and he was using one hand to press on her hip and the other to yank down her pants. A belt buckle jangled and Jared pulled her white cotton underpants aside, his weight rendering her immobile as he entered her. His lips pressed a hot breathy smut talk into her ear. When she finally wiggled from his grasp, Angie scratched at his face, both hands wheeling in fear that rose to panicky animal rage.

"*Son of a bitch*," Jared said. "What in the hell is *wrong* with you?" He caught her wrists in one hand and sat up, seething, hitching up his pants and shoving her to the floor.

Frantic, she scrambled for her clothes and popped to her feet, voice trembling.

"What *the heck*, Jared?" Her fingers trembled on zippers and buttons. "I've never been to *third base*, you asshole."

"Don't play innocent with me, you little *prick* tease," his eyes narrowed, cold. "You've been egging me on for years."

She clutched at her jacket, to hide the rip in her blouse, then she ran through the silent streets toward home as a dog barked in the distance. Heart pounding, she stopped to catch her breath. Where did she think she was going? Nowhere felt safe now. *You gotta get outta here,* she sobbed, gulping air. Where would she run? The only soul in Lewistown who'd believe her was Ada.

Her father Jacob Lovejoy was an incurious man, with thinning dirty blond hair, darting eyes, and an Adam's apple that bounced when he spoke, which wasn't often. Few could recall an opinion that strayed beyond Church teachings and, despite a lifetime spent in his hometown, he'd left no discernable trace. When she came, sobbing, Jacob lamented his daughter's lost chastity, calling it 'a prize you can never regain" quoting Church teachings. His eyes were fixed on the floor. "This will work itself out," he mumbled apologetically. "Jared's a good man. People make mistakes. Let's all just move on."

His words crushed Angie. Jacob Lovejoy would rather keep the peace than defend his own daughter. Angie never understood her parents' passivity, but the town was equally complicit. Everyone knew everyone's business, but were all too brainwashed to speak up.

Except of course, her grandmother. "Shoot him in the balls," Ada suggested, blue eyes widened. "Let the whole town watch him bleed out." At 63, widowed, Ada favored the old-fashioned cowboy eye-for-an eye approach to justice. "Lewiston," Ada explained, "is a cattle town on the road to nowhere, where men are a protected species, like bison and bald eagles – no harm will ever come to them."

"He couldn't look me in the eye," Angie wept to her grandmother. "*Your own son.* He might as well have said, *Sorry, shit happens, deal with it.* And Mother? You'd thought I'd shamed *her*. I can't do this Nana. I can't watch this town sweep a crime under the rug. You know that's exactly what they'll do. I'm marked for life here." Angie never understood her parents' passivity, but the town was equally complicit. Everyone knew everyone's business, but they were all too brainwashed to think, or speak up.

Ada fought back tears and gave her granddaughter a fierce hug and a smile. Angie's story was nothing new for Lewiston. For some families, rape brought such profound shame that murder was preferable. Folks used scripture to justify this twisted logic. Women were simply second-class citizens who took orders from the men. Ada understood. She'd married a man who casually screwed other women, his other wives, with no thought. Gas lit over generations, women turned the blame inward, to keep the peace, and their children. Leaving was unfathomable.

"Oh honey, you are so brave," Ada told her. "Don't stick around like I did. Get out of here, go to New York, chase your dreams, be a star." Ada saw potential in her tomboy granddaughter. If anyone could escape this life, it was Angie. "Go live like Holly Golightly," Ada told her, with wink. "And wear hats like Audrey Hepburn. Live it for me!"

Angie smiled, wiping away her tears with the back of her hand. "I needed you to tell me that," she sighed. "I could never go to my parents. But I don't know a soul in New York. And I've only got two hundred dollars in my savings account."

"Come over here," Ada motioned her to sit on the bench at the foot of her bed. "You'll be just fine. But you'll need these." She stood and crossed the room to her dresser, took an envelope from the top drawer, and counted ten crisp $100 bills. "I hear New York City is expensive." She handled her money nimbly, like a Vegas croupier. The bills had the inky cotton fragrance of new paper money. It smelled of sweet possibility; unlike the pulp mills of Lewiston.

Ada tucked the cash into an envelope and handed it to Angie. "There's a fine hotel there for women called the Barbizon. I have an old friend who stayed there back in the thirties." Angie was a child when movies came to Orchard's Auto Theatre on Bryden Avenue, expanding her world. Charmed by New York life, she'd watched 'Barefoot in the Park' and 'How to Marry a Millionaire.' Everyone was handsome and their lives were so interesting.

Now Angie would be a part of that -- her own Emerald City, to escape the stench of Lewiston. Her feeble-minded parents had chosen a duplicitous Savior over their own child. Some scars run deeper than the cut.

"I don't know what was worse," Angie told May. "Jared Bingham or my parents' reaction to what he did," Angie said softly, as if waking from a trance. "The Church and the hypocrisy in that *fucking town*. It's left me angry, even now. I made my own sort of peace with it, but time doesn't heal all wounds. Nothing was truly resolved. And the guy who ... *did that* ... to me now has a nice house, a wife, and a passel of kids. *Pillar* of the community." Angie took a deep breath. "I'm sorry. I thought I was over it. Guess not," she said softly. "I'm not usually this emotional."

Angie felt rich as she journeyed across the country in the late summer of 1966. She'd seen a $100 bill only once. Now, with eight on them tucked into a secret pouch in her purse, she felt liberated, thanks to Ada. Back in Lewiston, a gossip storm swirled in her wake. The whispers, all untrue, suggested she'd been knocked-up. Maybe by that baseball player, dragging Reggie Jackson into the scandal. If the truth was inconvenient, a whopper would have to do. In Lewiston, it came down to trashing the girl every time.

Even her family name, Angela Lovejoy, mocked her. Love and joy distorted into secrecy and duty to the Church of Latter Day Saints. Forgive, forget and obey, that was the deal. Still, how could they fail to *protect* her? Wasn't that every parent's job? Ada had scolded her son and daughter-in-law. "A grown man sexually assaulted your daughter," she said, pointing a finger at both of them, "and you're telling me that doesn't *bother* you?"

The blow up lingered in her mind. "Honey, boys will be boys," her mother said. "They need their women to support them. People make mistakes, and we're taught to forgive." But her dad's diffidence had really stunned her. "What kind of father *does nothing* when his only daughter is violated by a neighbor's son?

Angie's plaid Perma-Prest dress kept its shape on the cross-country journey. Except for a few stretches with a seatmate, she sat alone on the bus, extending her long legs into the aisle and gazing out of the window. Now, in the cab, she clutched the handle of a brown leather suitcase and gawked at the people walking along Forty-Second Street. The huge billboards and neon signs spelling Coca-Cola, Canadian Club whiskey, Castro Convertibles, and 'The Good, the Bad and the Ugly' thrilled her.

Lewiston's only billboard advertised the local car dealership. It was owned by her father's third cousin and read *You're Ahead in a Ford.* Here, a movie marquis flashed 'How to Steal a Million,' twenty-five cent peep shows touted 'private preview booths' and, across the street, Gwen Verdon was starring in 'Sweet Charity.'

Angie was gob smacked. In just one block, she'd seen more people and blinking electric lights than in all of Idaho. She'd heard that Times Square had gone downhill, overrun by prostitutes and riffraff. Still, she found the flashing advertisements fascinating. Maybe she'd find a job on Madison Avenue, where all those ads are thought up? She smiled at the idea of that. Why not?

A large woman, skin the color of mahogany, strolled on the arm of an older gentleman. Angie had seen only two Negros in the flesh on trips to Spokane with her grandma. The woman's silky red dress, with matching hat and purse, complimented her escort's natty blue suit and straw fedora. He marked each stride with a jaunty flick of his gold-tipped cane, as they walked together with the unhurried ease of royalty. Angie loved this flood of images and the people, all moving separately along sidewalks as wide as four-lane highways, their unspoken dance choreographed to the cadence of the traffic lights.

Angie's Checker cab crossed 42nd Street and turned left on Third Avenue, heading uptown. As they rolled north, the signs and office buildings gave way to apartment buildings, fine shops, and restaurants. Angie drank it all in: the signs, the cars, and the people, dressed stylishly and walking at a brisk pace. No one stopped to talk. You couldn't go fifty yards in Lewiston without running into a nosy relative. She liked seeing people in a hurry. She felt their impatience, too.

Four

"Miss, this is The Barbizon," the taxi driver punched the meter as he pulled to a stop. "You'll be in good hands here." Angie stepped onto the curb at 63rd and Lexington, marveling at the 23-story building faced in salmon-colored marble. Behind them, another driver honked, threw his hands in the air, and yelled something she couldn't make out.

The taxi driver sprung from the cab to yell back, gesturing wildly to send the car around him. Then he popped the trunk and reached for her suitcase, meeting her eyes and smiling gently. "That'll be $1.80, ma'am," he said. "I hear this is a nice place for nice girls. Good luck in New York City."

Grace Kelly and Tippi Hedren had lived at the Barbizon before their careers took off. So had *Titanic* survivor Molly Brown and the writer Sylvia Plath. "I've looked into it," Ada had told her. "You pay $35 a week. No liquor or men upstairs. And in the evenings, even the elevator operators are female. They think of everything. We just need two references. I've got a friend over in Spokane who lived there in the thirties," she explained excitedly. "She danced with the Ziegfeld Follies! I'll call her."

The Barbizon's lobby was even grander than the Owyhee Hotel's in Boise, famous for its rooftop garden with a dance floor, where a live band played on weekends. Back in the 1950s, her mother and grandmother would take Angie on the 300-mile drive to Boise to go shopping twice a year. Ada called these trips "sanity checks," a weekend pass for the inmates. The change of scenery did them all good; but these forays into the real world also showed them what Lewiston was missing.

New York was a hundred times the size of Boise. The Barbizon was surrounded by so many tall buildings that it looked small in comparison. Angie had seen it first in *Mademoiselle* magazine, in a full-page ad touting 'New York's Most Exclusive Hotel Residence for Young Women.' The women in the ad all looked smart and stylish. For the first time, Angie sensed she might have an identity all her own and, just maybe, she'd discover her own direction in life.

"I escaped, just like Nana and I planned," she announced, returning to her guests. "I took my future into my own hands. No one should have to do that at such a tender age, but I had no choice. Ada warned me about 'the wolves' who roamed New York; men on the lookout for pretty, naïve, young things. For someone stuck in rural Idaho, Ada had an unexpected worldliness about her."

Clara stepped through the doorway from the kitchen carrying a large pitcher of ice water with three plastic glasses. She placed them on the table as Angie continued. "Ada was the only adult willing to risk helping me. The rest turned away, as if I'd brought the rape on myself.

"The Barbizon felt like both a sanctuary and a launching pad, the two things I most wanted in life," Angie continued, pouring a glass of water with a nod of thanks to Clara. "I couldn't help looking around the lobby to see if I recognized anyone famous. Rita Hayworth was photographed there for *Life* magazine, in the gymnasium on the fifth floor."

Angie stood and took a few steps toward the deck railing. The birds had quieted, settling in the nearby treetops and ponds for the night. *Did I really need to go on so much about why I left Idaho?* Sexual abuse had quietly defined Angie's life, guiding each decision. She'd promised herself to be honest. No half-truths. But keep it light and entertaining. Clara had agreed: "You've lived a wild life," she reminded her. "So, make it worth reading. You'll inspire the next girl ..."

Angie spent much of the cross-country bus trip imagining who she might become once she arrived in New York. "Women in Idaho had babies. Simple as that," she snickered, reaching for her glass and taking a big sip of water. "I had no college degree and no marketable skills." The Katherine Gibbs Secretarial School occupied three floors of the Barbizon. She could always use that as a fall back.

The Dos Equis had left her feeling relaxed, ready to answer questions. Or she could just ramble on, which she was pretty good at too. "My only goal was to escape Lewiston and the Latter-Day Saints. That was a big enough decision for a twenty-one-year-old. Or a woman of *any* age.

At the time, I'd decided it was all my fault; I led Jared on, *blah, blah, blah*. I thought I could put it behind me if I moved away and built another life. It was all I could think to do.

"I was nervous approaching the lady at the front desk. But her bright smile put me at ease. Katherine Sibley introduced herself as the assistant manager, adding, 'And you are …?'

"Angela Lovejoy! I'd practiced sounding confident with Ada, but I felt like such a hick, wearing the skirt I left home in, after four days on a bus, no shower. I rummaged for the letters of introduction in my purse and, bless Katherine Sibley, she treated me like I was Grace Kelly herself."

"Oh yes, very *distinctive* name," she brightened. "Aspiring actress?"

"I told her I didn't know yet," Angie looked up at May and Clara, wide-eyed. "My first two hours in New York, and I'd been treated with more dignity than I'd ever known in Lewiston." How had that moment returned to her so vividly?

"She told me I was the first Idaho girl she'd ever met," Angie said, recalling she'd added, 'We have two young ladies here from California, one from Denver, and two sisters from Missoula, Montana.' "She spoke highly of my references, welcomed me, then she reached into a drawer and pulled out a typed sheet. 'As you would expect, we have rules about guests. Here's your copy. Just remember: No men above the lobby level. Welcome, Miss Lovejoy. We have you in room 322. Here is your key.'

Angie saw it clearly now, decades later. "Frumpy Miss Sibley was restoring my tattered spirit. She saw me. She treated me with kindness and respect. She proved to me that I mattered, just like anyone else."

Angie looked up at May and Clara, surprised at the fresh revelation. In escaping, she'd tapped into a deep reservoir of strength. She'd also discovered an uncanny knack for reading people. She'd chosen her taxi driver from a long line at the curb at Penn Station, hadn't she? She'd thought he looked kind. Now, as she recalled standing at the desk with Katherine Sibley, it clicked: Her first hours in New York, and already, she'd found allies.

Five

"When the porter handed me the key and left the room, I fell onto the bed and let out a sigh of relief. *'My key.'* I was stirred up and exhausted. New York felt friendly and scary, all at once."

They'd taken the elevator to the third floor. "There's a swimming pool, solarium and gymnasium on ten," the porter said, as he unlocked the door to the small, spotless room. Angie looked around, taking in the narrow bed, a dresser, floor lamp, and a small desk. The floral bedspread matched the draperies. He pulled a cord to part them and sunlight spilled in through two large windows facing Third Avenue.

"If you're hungry, " the porter continued, "there's a Horn & Hardart eight blocks south. A lot of girls like it. The food is homey, and the prices are reasonable." He set her suitcase on a rack in the closet and turned on the floor lamp, before taking his leave with a tip of his hat. "Please let us know if there is anything we can do to make your stay more enjoyable."

After the porter handed her the key and left the room, Angie collapsed onto the bed, tired but excited. Her feet tingled and her legs throbbed. She had stayed in a hotel just a few times before. This one had a library, formal recital rooms, and lounges for afternoon teas, nightly bridge games, and theatre readings. She felt like Eloise in The Plaza, as she closed her eyes. As cars honked and sirens blared below, she realized she was hungry.

"I had never been to an 'automat' before. I didn't even understand what it was." Horn & Hardart was a cavernous place crowded with people inserting coins into slots along a chrome and glass wall of small compartments containing freshly prepared meals. Men and women in black uniforms were continually stocking the space behind the glass windows and providing change for customers.

The large bustling hall was filled with lacquered tables. A ham-and-Swiss double-decker sandwich cost 45 cents. Fresh pumpkin pie was a quarter and a Fanta orange soda was another dime. Angie reckoned she could eat here for a year, if money was tight. "I instantly loved the choreography within this self-service world—an economy of movement that kept up the pace. No one seemed to know one another, unlike the restaurants back home.

"I deposited a handful of nickels and quarters in the slot and little doors opened like a county fair game. My entire meal cost under a dollar! As I turned, carrying my tray, I noticed an attractive young woman in black, her short bottle-blonde hair streaked with silver. Angie admired her earrings, shaped like chandeliers, and her eyes, rimmed in black and fanned with thick false eyelashes.

"Is anyone sitting there?" I asked. "I couldn't take my eyes off of her. She might have been a beautiful boy. After a long drag on her cigarette, she gestured to the table, inviting me to sit down. Then she smiled, pulled her coffee cup closer and returned to her glossy magazine.

"I slowly unloaded my tray, feeling like a bumpkin next to this chic New York woman, who must be a model. Her eyebrows were thick and dark; but she wore no lipstick. The effect was striking."

"New here?" she said with a warm smile. "When did you arrive?"

"Would you believe this morning?" Angie said, blushing. "Is it that obvious?" The woman looked to be in her mid-twenties.

"It's okay. I can tell these things," she shrugged, lips curling into a mischievous smile. "Takes one to know one. Where from?"

"Idaho," Angie answered shyly.

"I'm from California," she said cheerfully, putting her magazine down. "I'm Edie." She extended her graceful right hand. Her nails were long but natural, like the woman in the TV ad for Palmolive.

"I'm Angie. It's nice to meet a fellow westerner. You must be a model."

"Always *trying*," Edie answered, eyes brightening with a shrug. "I do a little acting too. Anything to keep the wolf from the door."

Angie instantly liked this striking stranger who drank coffee and lit up one cigarette after the other. Caffeine and tobacco were taboo back home. Edie smoked like a movie star. But her face, warm and friendly, told Angie they were more alike than she'd imagined.

"My father used to drag us to Sun Valley for vacations. It took us two full days to get there from Santa Barbara. So where in Idaho?"

"Well, at least there's snow in Sun Valley," Angie chuckled. "I'm from a river town called Lewiston in the middle of nowhere with a small hill and paper mills. Are you a skier?"

"Not a particularly good one," Edie replied laughing. "I like ice skating better, but it's been a few years since I've been on skates."

Angie had never met anyone like Edie. "What kind of acting do you do?"

"Well, that's a good question," Edie took a drag of her cigarette, exhaled, and chuckled. "The movies are experimental. Andy calls them *avant-garde*. The studio is ten blocks away. You should come by and see it."

"I'd love that," Angie answered, still wondering about the kind of movies they were making. 'Annie Get Your Gun' or 'Hello Dolly' didn't seem to fit Edie's look. She'd mentioned an *Andy*. Andy *who*?

May placed her palm over her forehead. "Stop. No. *Andy Warhol? You worked with Andy Warhol and Edie Sedgwick back in the heyday? Seriously?* I saw some pictures in *Vogue*.

They were *it* in 1966, the epitome of cool, art, style and rebellion." She'd read about Warhol in particular. May had been a Velvet Underground fan in college and she'd pieced together their histories over the past month. Edie was a visual icon of that era, the *It Girl* of her day, although not much of an actress.

"Edie told me to come by any afternoon," Angie answered, laughing. "Their workday was usually in swing by four … five, at the earliest. The Factory was over on 47th and Third, fifth floor. Edie said to take the freight elevator. They were starting to film a movie called 'Vinyl.'

"See you soon, I hope," Edie said, as she stood to leave, sliding dark sunglasses over her nose. As she waltzed out into a beautiful autumn afternoon, every man in the room looked up to watch. "It was an Idaho kind of day, clear without a drop of humidity," Angie recalled. "My first day in the big city, and I'd met Edie Sedgwick at the Automat. I was walking on air."

Angie flipped over the crisp Barbizon stationary, retrieved from the accordion file, the paper stock substantial and sophisticated thirty years later. "I felt like a celebrity sitting next to Edie," Angie laughed. "Once she left, everyone turned back to their fried liver and bacon and deep-fried sea scallops. No one seemed to notice the gawky girl from Idaho, who sat across from her." She shrugged with a smile. "Still, that day was magic."

"What a shame Horn & Hardart shut down," May said. "That was my first New York memory. It was such a cool place."

"Time marches on, doesn't it? New York was full of possibilities back then. AIDS changed all that, and then crack came along. The city hardened. Being an artist became a liability, rather than an asset. It was all about money, after that point." Angie thrust a letter at May, as if proving her point. "God was I innocent!"

September 11, 1968

Dear Nana:

I just arrived today in New York City! The Barbizon is amazing. It's so nice and everyone is friendly. I went to an automat and met a model from California. Her name is Edie. I saw someone on the street who looked like Ethel Merman. I hear you run into all kinds of celebrities here.

The bus trip across the country was neat, but boring. There's not much to see between Spokane and Chicago. I went to the Art Institute like you suggested and ate a big Chicago pizza. Had enough left over for breakfast and lunch on the bus. I also found out that there is a secretary school on the fifth floor of this hotel! What will they think of next?

But I've done it, just like we talked about. I feel like I am standing at the beginning, my year zero with my entire life ahead of me. I can't wait to try new things and I promise to make level-headed decisions. I will write you next week. Miss you!

All my love and thank you,

Angie

Angie rubbed her arms against the afternoon chill. "It's getting to be cocktail hour, sacred in late husband's family. Would you like a beer or glass of wine? Or something warm? A cup of tea? I'm a terrible host. Way out of practice. But I've earned myself a cold beer."

"I'd love some hot tea," May answered, picking up her pad and the cassette deck. "This is like a scene from a movie, Mrs. deGraaf. I can't believe you met Edie Sedgwick on your first day in New York."

They'd gotten off to a good start. Talking to reporters was always a crapshoot. Even now, she wasn't sure what was newsworthy – and what to keep private.

Six

"Looking for work?" The man barely glanced from his clipboard, but a light meter hung from a cord around his neck and his face looked gaunt. "We need production assistants. Start today if you want. Pay is $4 an hour, cash. What's your name?"

"Don't tell me …," May almost dropped her pencil. *"Billy Name?* At Warhol's *factory?"*

Downtown's youthful *avant garde* gravitated to Warhol's Silver Factory. The former hat-making workroom in midtown served as Andy's film studio. Edie had scribbled the address inside a matchbook saying, "Come by and see what's up." Angie had flipped the matchbook between her fingers for days, trying to gather the nerve to seek out the East 47th Street address.

"No one ever found success without taking a few risks," Ada counseled. "Live a little. Try new things. Just keep your wits about you." Her grandmother's words guided her steps along Third Avenue, passing under the Tinker Toy scaffoldings on a side street, before she sized up the steel door numbered 237. *Do it*, she whispered, shushing the urge to turn back to the Barbizon.

Angie would have turned tail and headed back to Idaho without Ada pressing her on. She plucked a letter from the bulging accordion file. Even now, they radiated with Ada's love. Twenty five years, gone in an instant. She mailed the last one with a ten-cent Robert Frost stamp almost two decades ago. Lately, the letters had fallen out of order, but Angie never failed to slip each letter back into its envelope after reading it.

When she couldn't scrape up the money for stationery and stamps, she'd buy aerograms; a quarter each, postage included. "I sent this one after I met Edie," she said, pointing to the first. "Then I met Andy."

Angie hesitated as she pushed through the door into the dimly-lit lobby, where the aroma of mildew and urine preceded the creaking elevator, which landed with a gentle thud. On four, she could hear the jangly beat of *Nowhere to Run* by Martha Reeves and the Vandellas' blaring, even before the door opened onto a vast loft space punctuated by six columns.

Two floor-to-ceiling windows cast a hazy light through the dusty peach fuzz that clung to every surface. Three men, lit by spotlights, stood arguing on a small stage, one flailing a hand-held camera. Angie scanned the space for Edie. A silver payphone hung on a far wall, near a makeshift darkroom. Beneath it, inexplicably, a running toilet was also painted silver.

"Yes, *yes, yes!*" a slight man wearing tinted glasses shouted over the noise. Pale and pockmarked, with a shock of blond hair, he looked to Angie like a cardboard corpse, with a miniscule frame and blue and white horizontal striped shirt. Still the actors and stagehands hung on his words, rapt. These factory walls held stories. Hats had gone out of style when President Kennedy took office. What else had they seen?

Her eye caught Edie's silver-streaked beehive, bringing a wave of relief. Edie was sitting on a steamer trunk, smoking a cigarette, and sipping from a white paper cup while a man pointed to a page in the script, explaining her upcoming scene. As she stood, she tugged at the leopard belt cinching her black tank dress, then caught Angie's eye, flashed a bright smile and waved her over.

"It was the strangest place I'd ever been," she told May and Clara. "Mind you, I'd never been beyond Spokane Washington. I'd heard of Andy Warhol, but his movies were strange, really strange without plots. No one took them seriously, other than Andy. They hired me on the spot. No interview, no resume. Hard to turn that down." She giggled, shaking her head at the memory.

"Billy!" Edie grabbed Angie's hand and tugged her toward the man with the light meter, slipping her arm through his crooked elbow. "This is the girl I told you about. Angie, right?" she said, bouncing to the beat as she made introductions. "Glad you are here."

Photographer Billy Name had been romantically linked to Warhol for a brief spell, and was serving as his cinematographer. "It's about a young vigilante named Victor, who spends his days lifting weights," he explained intently, dark eyes darting, "and his nights dancing and torturing people. We're trying to adapt 'A Clockwork Orange' to the stage, remade on film."

Angie couldn't fathom turning a movie into a play, only to film the play for a movie, but the hourly pay appealed. She extended her hand, shouting over the music, "Happy to help! Edie was nice enough to invite me." Billy Name's urgency seemed at odds with the cast, most of whom stood around bumming cigarettes.

A bearded man stood high on a wobbly extension ladder, hanging large, silk-screened images on the wall. He was clearly ticked off about something. Angie made a mental note to avoid ladders as Edie took her place near the steamer trunk, closed her eyes, and entered a languorous trance, swaying to the song. 'That's it, *that's it*," Billy yelled. "Perfect!"

Angie wasn't sure who Billy was talking to, but it didn't matter. The cast pulsated to the music as the camera lingered on Edie, hypnotic in her black tank dress, arms overhead. She never uttered a line, but Edie's star quality was palpable. Whatever was going on at The Factory, Angie wanted in.

Her first task, hanging a silver scrim along the back of the small stage, put her at the top rung of a ladder. Still, Angie felt overjoyed at landing a job. After rent this month, she'd have $225 left to her name. Andy had directed more than 100 films over the past five years. From shorts to hours-long reels, none would be mistaken for 'Breakfast at Tiffany's.' Plot, dialogue, and characters were scant; and she'd yet to see torture — or even weightlifting.

"I was a sponge, taking in every detail," Angie said as she filled the kettle and turned up the flame on the stove. "I fell in with Edie's friends, all artists and actors. And Andy! He had a peculiar charisma. The downtown artists fell over themselves to appear in his movies, and the uptown art patrons paid ridiculous prices for his portraits. He was a marketing genius, driving demand through his own carefully curated artistic mystique. *But boy was he an oddball!*"

After she'd mailed several letters about her film job, Ada wired tuition money for the Katherine Gibbs Secretarial School's Entrée program. The 11-week boot camp met until 3 p.m. daily, with homework each night. In addition to the $1775 enrollment fee, Ada added $200 to cover the required white gloves (two pairs), hat, skirts (three, knee length), and moderate heels. Dress boots were sanctioned in winter; clogs and sandals were forbidden.

Thus began Angie's double life, which swung like a pendulum from prim corporate trainers to this band of artsy misfits who danced in silver minidresses and lounged naked in Lucite bathtubs. In her letters to Ada, she emphasized the prim side, glossing over her movie job. She didn't want her grandmother to worry. Although edgy, Angie felt safe at The Factory. Plus they paid promptly, if not lavishly. She didn't want her grandmother to worry.

The hours dovetailed too. Her classes ended each day at 3 p.m., at least an hour before the Factory was cranking to life. Plaques placed around the Gibbs classroom exhorted students to 'Stand above the crowd' and show 'Excellence in all you do.' She chuckled at the irony. Wasn't the hefty tuition motivation enough?

"If I'd wanted to be a secretary, I could have stayed in Boise," she said, winking at Clara. "But I had to do *something*. I had no college degree; I was just dumb labor. And four dollars an hour wasn't going to cut it for long. With an office job, at least I'd have a salary, health insurance and, a chance to get somewhere."

Katie Gibbs insisted students prepare for job interviews, getting their spiel down pat. "What are your strengths?" her teachers asked. "Where do you see yourself in five years? Ten years? You'll be nervous, but if you're prepared, you'll sound professional. You have the skills; now *show them*! Project success! *Smile!* Keep your hands off your face when you talk. Our alumna have gone on to run banks and edit magazines. We are *professional* trainers for *successful* women."

Angie felt little kinship with the lady go-getters at Katie Gibbs. Sweet and serious girls, their dreams began and ended with landing a husband or a job at the Metropolitan Life Insurance Company. "They were all about corporate ladders and 'making it,'" she laughed. "I couldn't think of anything worse than moving to New Rochelle with the man of my dreams. New York had more to offer. That much I *did* know."

When a secretarial job at Young & Rubicam turned up on the Gibbs bulletin board, she felt a frisson of hope. "I was thinking an advertising agency offered a mix of corporate and creative," Angie reasoned. "Maybe not as creative or fun as what Edie and Andy were doing, but with a starting salary at $115 a week, plus benefits, it was worth a shot."

Angie dialed Y&R from the Barbizon's fifth-floor phone booth and Olivia Glynn picked up. "We look for high quality support staff," she intoned in a posh English accent. "Ad agencies aren't known for their buttoned-up behavior, so we trust our administrative assistants to set the proper tone with our clients." Glynn's voice turned from crisp to sunny. "Why don't we have a chat? Could you come in for an interview on Tuesday?"

A week later, Angie peered into the mirror, rehearsing her lines as she pulled her hair back and zipped up her simple navy dress. Would Miss Glynn notice her inexperience, like the lace edge of a slip? As she took a seat in her office, she was careful to cross her ankles, place her purse on the chair beside her, and remove her white gloves, before cheerfully recounting her desire "to work in the business end of a creative field."

The phrasing struck a serious but open-ended tone, she and Ada had agreed. If she was going to spend her days typing, an ad agency beat an insurance company. If Marsh and McLennan was elevator music, Y&R was Woodstock.

"Nice turn of phrase, young lady," Miss Glynn broke into a smile as she scanned Angie's wafer-thin resume.

"Have you heard of our *Wings of Man* campaign? Eastern Airlines?" Miss Glynn set the resume aside. "We're looking for an assistant to the creative director on the account."

Angie nodded. She'd seen the sophisticated Whisper Jet ads on TV and now felt as if she'd fallen in with the big-city girls. "It's a highly visible job, very high-pressure," Miss Glynn continued.

Miss Glynn then took off her glasses, placing them on her desk. "But I must warn you, Miss Lovejoy. Mr. Caputo can be difficult at times. He's extremely talented, but a bit mercurial, as our best executives can be. To that end, I do feel obliged to disclose that he's gone through three assistants in two years." She sighed, offering a sisterly eye roll.

If Angie heard warning bells, the prospect of a pay check silenced them. Miss Glynn had trusted her with this salacious tidbit, so Angie would return the favor and tame the talented Mr. Caputo. She'd managed Andy, hadn't she?

"I'm familiar with difficult men," she told Miss Glynn, choosing her words carefully. "I grew up in a Mormon community in Idaho."

Seven

As Angie left her job interview at Young and Rubicam on the East Side, across town at the Brill Building, Artie Mogull stood before his Steinway and pressed the middle C. The piano, one of two baby grands in the music executive's sprawling fifth-floor office, struck a note as sour as his mood. He'd need to call a tuner. Artie had a damn good ear if you didn't already know.

The single sour note would set the musical planets in motion. From the Brill Building to The Bronx to the East Village, it would trigger a chain reaction, unleashing a sound that, in time, would reverberate around the world.

Whether or not Artie deserved this stroke of luck was another question entirely. As an 'artists and repertory man,' known in the trade as A&R, Artie Mogull was legendary for discovering the raw talent that yielded hit songs. He'd entered the music rights business straight out of Columbia after the war, working for a company his cousin had founded, catching the wave of success and riding it out for the past twenty years.

But today, Artie felt only aggravation. He picked up the Yellow Pages and slapped it open on his desk, flipping the pages in search of a piano tuner. He landed on Lou Nigro. A musician himself. Nigro played clubs, weddings, and bar mitzvahs. When Nigro received the call, he recognized the name instantly.

"Of course, I've heard of your work. People say nice things about you. Carole King is a gift to the world," Nigro answered.

"I like opportunities for us old schlumps," he continued from his Bronx apartment. "I'm coming into town this afternoon for some other clients. I could swing by around four o'clock if that suits your schedule?" Nigro could fix any old piano, but today he had another mission in mind. He grabbed his coat and satchel of tools before he hung up the phone, then he shot out the door, headed for the downtown subway.

When his secretary rapped her knuckle on his office door, Mogull barely glanced up from his desk at the piano tuner. "It's the Steinway on the right," he said, in no mood for small talk. "And while you're here, check the other one, too, would ya?"

Nigro got to work, biding his time, as Artie made a few phone calls. He chewed out two producers, smoothed the ruffled feathers of a pop star, then left a message for his tailor. As the A&R man cooled off a bit, Nigro tested his luck. "So, what kinds of acts do you represent?" he said, trying to sound nonchalant.

"Talented ones who make money," Artie snapped, irritated. "Got a young Jewish guy from Minnesota. Bob Dylan. Heard of him?"

"Sure," Nigro volunteered, then nudged a bit further. "Anyone else I know?"

"Just *tune* the goddamn piano." Artie Mogull had no interest in chatting up this schmuck.

Nigro remained calm, biding his time, waiting for the right moment.

"My daughter writes songs," he said eventually, to no one in particular. "*Good* ones, too," he held the note an extra beat. "Better than a lot of the sing-songy crap that comes out of this building."

Mogull just wanted his piano tuned. "Solid gold crap," he tossed back annoyed. If he'd been aggravated before, now he was downright hostile. "You heard of Carole King? Ellie Greenwich? Cynthia Weil? I took those girls *to the fuckin' moon* and back. Carole was seventeen years old when she wrote 'Will You Love Me Tomorrow?' for The Shirelles. So, I'll excuse your rude question. A lot of *good* crap comes out of this building every day." Artie caught himself, recalibrated. "Particularly out of this office. So what's your daughter done?"

"Nothing … yet." Nigro's measured calm held the precise note of indifference that neutralized Artie's bluster.

"I'm not just saying this because she's my daughter. I believe she has unusual talent."

"Really? That's bullshit and you know it. Look buddy, I don't want to argue with you." He paused, taking a deep breath, seeing an opportunity. "Tell you what. Bring her in tomorrow at 10 am. I'll give her fifteen minutes. And, for my trouble time and generosity, this job's on *you*. No charge. The piano better be pitch perfect. Fair enough, bubbe?" He glared at Nigro before extending his meaty hand. "Deal?"

The piano tuner nodded slowly, leaning forward to shake Mogull's hand. "Okay then. Now if you'll excuse me, I've got a meeting across town," he lied, as he grabbed his coat and headed for the door. "My secretary will see you out. Good day."

Nigro turned up at 1619 Broadway the next morning with his daughter. A dumpy teenager, short and pale, she wore a gauzy black dress and a large knit cloche. *So much for putting her on stage*, thought Mogull, sizing up the young girl who didn't smile, nor seem interested in being a pop star. The girl offered him a sweaty handshake, introducing herself simply as Laura, unsmiling. *He sure as hell wasn't going to put her on stage in a mini skirt.* She showed little interest in pop stardom and she'd dressed the part. Even her long hair was parted unfashionably on the side.

Artie gestured toward the Steinway and the girl took the piano bench, shifted a bit, placed her fingers on the keys, and closed her eyes. Over the next fifteen minutes, Lou Nigro's daughter played 'Stoney End', 'And When I

Die', 'Eli's Coming,' and 'Wedding Bell Blues' straight through, looking up only when she'd finished.

Mogull stood dumbstruck, astounded. "You wrote those tunes? By yourself? Really? *Wow!* The chord structures are unusual. The bar variations, from one song to the next. And the lyrics are yours, too? It all sounds so new, progressive, but familiar. You're talented, kiddo. *How old are you?*"

"Nineteen," she answered softly.

"Ever played with a big orchestra behind you?" Artie was smiling now, nodding as he tamped out his cigarette. "You're not the greatest singer I've ever heard, but there's something ... yeah, I'll take a bop at you. But first, we have to do something with your name. You're not a R&B act, so it's confusing."

"What about my name, sir?" she asked. A Bronx-born Italo-Ukrainean Jew, Nigro had never questioned her surname. She tilted her head. But before she could protest, her father shot her a glare, cutting her off with a sharp hand thrust.

"Go with Nyro or Nero," Artie said, wheels turning. Nyro's probably better, no confusion with the actor in 'Camelot.' It's just easier to promote. And no one one will confuse you with the colored girls from Motown. Any other songs?"

"No," she answered, confused.

"Know any pop songs?" Artie tried again. "'Stardust?' 'Moon River?'"

"Yeah, I know some of them. And a few other songs. A few lines from each one, maybe."

"There's Irving Berlin."

The girl broke into a sly smile, meeting Artie's eyes. "And there's Bob Dylan."

"Oh yeah?" Mogull said, practically giddy now. "I know that guy. Helped getting him started, too. Do you know any pop standards?"

"Misty," she was feeling at ease now. "And 'When Sunny Get Blue." She struck a few chords of the Johnny Mathis hit and sang a few bars. Then searching for another key, she launched into the Leiber-Stoller classic 'Kansas City', but stopped abruptly. She didn't know the piano accompaniment to that one either.

Finally she took a stab at Dusty Springfield, singing *a cappella*. 'I don't know what it is that makes me love you so … it's crazy but it's true, I only want to be with you.'

"You are a piece of work, young lady," Artie announced proudly, as if he's raised her himself. "An original for sure," he laughed. "You've got some talent. I've never seen anything quite like you," he continued, noticing the purple nail polish on her stubby fingers. "There's more Broadway and Tin Pan Alley than rock 'n roll in you. How we best get your music out is something to think about." He looked toward the shy woman with the belting voice, imagining her songs playing on the radio, burning up the charts, just sung by someone ... else.

"This girl needs an agent," Mogull continued excitedly. "I'll call Milt." All he could think about was her talent and the need to find someone to perform the songs. Maybe Johnny Mathis or Barbra Streisand? he thought to himself. *This girl has the goods, she's a hitmaker, but the voice is untrained. She gets screechy on the high notes. No stage presence.*

Lou Nigro stood back and beamed. His daughter had been banging out melodies on the family piano since she was ten. She played everything, even a little Klezmer around the holidays. He never realized until that point how talented his *bubeleh* was. She was a rare gem every agent dreams of discovering.

"So what's next?" he asked, trying to suppress the pride dwelling in his heart. He'd tuned the piano one day and the next, his daughter was landing an agent. She could get a record deal. Nigro or Nyro, what did it matter? Still who would confuse his Jewish daughter with a colored R&B singer?

"Let's get her an agent, bring in some backup musicians, see what she sounds like," Artie was getting excited now. "Those compositions of hers can carry a lot of instruments. And of course, she'll need some management, recording and publishing contracts. Did you say she wrote these songs when she was fifteen? That's *insane!* Let me call Milt. Can you two come in tomorrow?"

Milt Okum was the man everyone wanted in their corner to launch a music career. Described as 'a producer who looks like an accountant and an accountant who looks like a producer,' Okum ran Cherry Lane Music Publishing out of his East Village apartment. Peter Paul and Mary were current clients and Artie Mogull could already tell that this awkward girl from College Street along the Grand Concourse with charming, rangy melodies, evocative imagery and intricate internal rhymes was special … and utterly mesmerizing. A talent like this emerged once in a blue moon.

Her voice had an enticing 'ping' he had heard in great opera singers, but she mumbled through the refrains and would be a lousy performer. Too introverted and zero sex appeal. A few of the songs meandered and went on too long. "A diamond in the rough, that's what she is, but we're gonna polish her up," he thought excitedly. "What a talent!

Laura Nyro had arrived in his office not by plan or design, but through a series of ordinary events, none of which seemed particularly consequential: An off-key piano, a listing in the Yellow Pages, a game of mental chess between her father, a patient piano tuner, and himself, a damn good talent spotter. The sheer serendipity left Artie awestruck. Now, before him, stood 19-year-old Laura Nyro. He'd found his Holy Grail: a female Bob Dylan.

Eight

"All right everyone, mark your calendars," Christian clapped his hands as his junior account executives at Ogilvy & Mather filed into the conference room. "Porgy and Bess' is coming to The Met in November. Trust me, It is the *only* opera you ever need to see live. Rigoletto and the rest? Expensive naps, *completely* unintelligible."

If his rising stars were going to tap into the *zeitgeist*, they'd need to draw on a rich cultural foundation. Christian possessed an encyclopedic knowledge of music; from opera to gospel, bubblegum, pop, and jazz. He'd tasked himself with educating his youthful colleagues. "You never know," he'd say, blue eyes twinkling. "Today's unknown anthem might be tomorrow's catchy jingle."

Ogilvy's Hathaway shirt man made the black eye patch sexy, putting the agency on the map. Christian oversaw four of their General Foods accounts, creating campaigns for Maxwell House coffee and Post children's cereals. A natural talent, he'd risen through the ranks quickly. Christian welcomed the inevitable *what do you do?* question at cocktail parties. Everyone knew his ads -- and who could resist a cartoon bear who crooned like Bing Crosby about sugary cereal?

By five o'clock on most afternoons, he'd poke his head into an office or two with a flirtatious come on: "Anyone for Maggie's? I'm not buying, but I do approve expense reports."

For as long as he could remember, Christian's mother had poured a martini on the rocks every afternoon well before dusk. The cocktail hour was sacred at the deGraaf home on 89th Street off Madison. His father Isaac never touched 'the olive soup' before 6:01 each evening. He'd follow his martini with a single glass of wine over dinner before retreating to his study to work.

May laughed. "I saw photos of them in the society pages. Sounds like your in-laws were the original power couple." She flipped through her notebook looking for the clipping.

"I was a rube from Idaho, for heaven's sake," Angie explained. "Isaac and Marge welcomed me into their fancy lives, just as they'd done with Christian's nanny, Duella. They just folded us into the family. I loved them for that."

"How did you two meet?" May asked.

"I met Christian in Jamaica. The tourism board had flown me to Kingston to make a commercial. By some complete lark, Christian happened to be there with Carlos. I liked them both; I assumed they were gay. But we became good friends. After that, he'd call from time to time. We'd go to dinner in the city – just friends," Angie noted. "We didn't get together until a few years later, maybe 1978? It was complicated, to say the least. But Isaac and Marge never judged me."

"Was it true that Isaac quietly ran the city in the 'sixties?" May asked. "I know Mrs. deGraaf was big on the charity ball circuit."

Around Gracie Mansion, Isaac deGraaf was known as 'The Dutch Master.' He was among a dying breed of Liberal Party New Yorkers who'd led the city through the boom-boom fifties. A genius with numbers, Isaac lacked Christian's charisma but shared his lanky frame. "He reminded me of a dour scarecrow badly in need of a tailor," Angie laughed. "His wrists always dangled well past his suit cuffs."

John Lindsay was elected New York's mayor in 1966. "By the time I arrived a year later, the city was already beginning to fray at the seams," Angie noted. Every year, Lindsay would proclaim the city's budget had reached a crisis point. Then he'd sink into more debt to sidestep battles over his progressive agenda.

"This can't go on, John," Isaac implored. "The numbers don't add up. Public sector growth at 80 percent? It's irresponsible. You're asking for a recession." With each corporate tax hike, Fortune 500 companies were pulling up stakes, leaving the city in droves, 55 at last count. Among the city's 121 breweries, Shaeffer, Rheingold, Schlitz, and Piels had already moved away.

Corporations weren't the only casualties. As income taxes nearly doubled, even dyed-in-the-wool New Yorkers were fleeing to Connecticut or the Sun Belt. "This isn't musical chairs, John. The next administration will inherit a very sick city that no one wants to treat." Isaac had been staving off financial crises for years, but even the Dutch Master couldn't hold his finger in the dam forever. When the city went broke a decade later, it was a wonder it hadn't happened sooner.

Christian's mother hailed from Chicago, an heiress to the Marshall Field department store fortune. She'd come to New York to attend Barnard in the thirties and never left. At five foot ten, Marge was outsized in more than stature. Family intimates called her 'Large Marge in Charge," but never within earshot. She smoked Marlboros, drank bourbon and had a knack for dropping phrases like *municipal borrowing* into conversations, just to get a rise out of her workaholic husband.

On his 15th birthday, Marge took Christian to Bergdorf's to pick out his first tuxedo. Once suitably dressed, he became her social escort, attending the charity galas that tried her husband's patience. By his 20s, Christian had grown to love gossip, attention and cheap Sauvignon Blanc. He'd talk passionately about new music, exotic destinations, clever ads and Broadway openings, wine glass in hand.

Christian could turn up at a white-tie ball one night, dive bar the next. Marge's socialite friends adored him. He returned their subtle flirtations with his own playful grand gestures; kissing an outstretched hand, admiring a diamond bauble, or naming the designer behind "that *stunning* dress

… you look like a *goddess.*" His exaggerated fawning was all in fun. Or was it? Christian would shoot a private wink across a crowded ballroom, just to keep the women guessing.

After Princeton, his father suggested he apply to law school or meet with one of his Wall Street friends about a banking job. "Do something befitting your station in life," he exhorted his son. With privilege came the obligation to serve, Isaac believed. Christian fervently agreed with his father. In theory.

"Family dinners could be tough sledding," Angie said. "To escape home and defer any career decisions, Christian traveled through New Guinea with Michael Rockefeller for six months. He'd grown up three blocks from the Rockefeller's townhouse, falling in the family as their unofficial fifth child."

"We *need* a sense of humor on this trip," Michael had pleaded. "Please say you'll come, Christian." It didn't take much to twist his arm.

The Dutch hadn't bothered to colonize New Guinea with its violent tribal cultures, five hundred plus languages, monkey-eating eagles, raging rivers and snow-capped mountains. Instead, they unloaded its abundant natural hazards on Australia, becoming a protectorate in the 1920s until its independence in 1975.

In New Guinea, the group was stunned to encounter a tribe of small, stocky dark men who carried stone axes and looked equally stunned at their white intruders. Their feathered headdresses featured colorful Bird of Paradise, but otherwise clothing was not a priority. "Nothing but penis gourds and ass grass," Christian reported, as if he'd spent a weekend in the Poconos.

"He traveled the way he lived," Angie said, nodding towards the bookshelf, "Fearless and unapologetic. Some people bring home Italian pottery. Christian collected Stone Age dildos and tribal war masks."

After his 'walkabout', Christian returned to New York feeling adrift. "You can't postpone adulthood indefinitely," Isaac had chided. But the grim prospect of working for a law firm or a bank took the spark right out of him.

When Michael returned to New Guinea the following year, Christian politely declined his invitation. It was the last time he'd speak to the childhood friend he loved like a brother. Not long after he arrived back in New Guinea, Michael promptly vanished. When extensive searches over several years proved fruitless, he was declared dead in 1964. Some say he was taken by cannibals; but Christian insisted it was an accidental drowning. Either way, the loss of his friend was devastating.

When he finally felt up to venturing out again, he saw Robert Morse on Broadway in the 1961 production of *How to Succeed in Business Without Really Trying*. Morse's character, J. Pierpont Finch captured Christian's imagination. By the time the curtain fell, Finch had become Christian's role model.

Granny's dough would kick in once Christian turned 25. Until then, a stint in advertising would patch him through. While many of his Princeton classmates stepped into their fathers' shoes, Christian remained content to do as he pleased.

Nine

Miss Glynn roared, slapping her leg. "That's a good one, Miss Lovejoy. So, Idaho has its share of difficult men, too? You're the first I've hired from there, but you'll do fine here at Young & Rubicam. I can tell you're a Gibbs girl with ambition, and I mean that in the best possible way. When can you start?"

"Thank you, ma'am," Angie felt her cheeks flush. "I could start tomorrow."

"How's next week?"

"I thought I'd won the lottery," Angie said, remembering that moment like it was yesterday. "But I hadn't come all that way to type letters from Steve Caputo. I thought I could handle him, but I should have listened to Miss Glynn's warning."

Dear Nana:

My new boss at the advertising agency is a guy from Teaneck, New Jersey. He wears tunic shirts like the ones in Dr. Zhivago, ha ha. He'd married with three kids, but I think he's got a girlfriend on the side. It's none of my beeswax, I know.

I still help out at The Factory. They're really nice there, even though some of them have tattoos and wear weird clothes. The movies are kinda silly, but harmless. My friend Edie from California looks out for me there. She's an actress and a model, but she'd really sweet; not stuck up like you might think. I guess I'm attracted to oddballs, and that's all your fault.

Love you Nana, Angie

"Goodness, you must be hungry!" Angie paused, remembering her manners. "I bought lobster salad at the market. Clara can tell you, I'm not much of a cook. But I have some Brie and crackers, too. It's getting chilly, so let's go inside and get the wood stove going. My dear father-in-law refused to install baseboard heat, or even insulation."

"I'll get it," Clara volunteered, hopping up. "It's getting juicy soon. The Warhol movie …" she teased. "What a nightmare! We can laugh about it now."

Angie lit the pot belly stove and set out throw blankets for her guests. "Have a seat over there," she pointed toward the lumpy sofa. May looked up with a bright smile. Musicians could be prickly. But so far, Mrs. deGraaf had been candid, clear-headed, and quick to look her in the eye and admit her mistakes.

The memory of Steve Caputo, bearded and barrel-chested, stirred up a peculiar shame that Angie thought was behind her. She'd navigated New York's fringes quite ably, but the corporate world proved far trickier.

"Young and stupid, what can I say? For a good four months, Steve was charming and polite. I'd learned to pump him up, feed his outsized ego. When the flowers started coming, I should have picked up on it. On the first of each month, I'd find a beautiful arrangement on my desk with a note: "Keep up the good work, Angela. You are a real asset to my team."

Clara returned with a tray. Hot tea for May. Two bottles of Dos Equis for her and Angie. And a platter with lobster salad, cheese, crackers, sliced deli ham and a baguette. "Where was I?" Angie continued, spreading brie on Ritz crackers and passing the platter around to her guests. The logs had caught fire in the stove and the chilly room had begun to feel cozy.

"I answered his phone, took messages, and typed his expense reports. Mostly I made reservations at the Four Seasons. He never mentioned who was joining him and I never asked. Katie Gibbs preached discretion. We drew a strict line between work and home. But I doubt he was entertaining clients on Sundays at 6 p.m."

In addition to the 'Wings of Man' campaign, Steve Caputo had written 'Let Your Fingers Do the Walking' and 'I Wish I Were an Oscar Mayer Wiener.' The bookshelf in his office was lined with Clios, Effys, and other awards; jagged engraved glass sculptures confirming his successes. Whenever Angie stepped into his office to leave a phone message slip or piece of mail on his desk, she felt proud to work for an industry superstar. He was polite too, asking about her hometown, family and interests.

At Y&R, few people cared for him. But nobody could deny his uncanny ear for arresting ideas and spot-on slogans. From a turgid brand strategy brief, he could elevate dish soap into a rare collectible. In return, he expected star treatment from anyone who crossed his path.

Miss Glynn was right. Steve was 'mercurial.' He once called Oscar Mayer's senior client 'ridiculous,' for questioning a headline. He blew up at colleagues, dominated meetings, and exhausted anyone within earshot with his claims of important Italian heritage, despite his New Jersey accent.

Still his rough edges were softened by an occasional self-deprecating comment, and his penetrating brown eyes gave Steve Caputo a coarse magnetism. On his desk, he displayed photographs of his sons, Rocco and Tony. He had a daughter, Lucia, too, who she'd met just once.

Angie called his wife Carmen a few times, offering excuses to cover his dalliances. His wife had never set foot in the city and Steve yielded scant evidence that she existed. He kept an apartment at the Roosevelt Hotel, five blocks up Madison at 45th Street. Steve would stay in town several nights a week, claiming he was 'working late.'

"Advertising was fun back then. Christian always said the MBA suits ruined it, but I loved the work," Angie reminisced. "Most people were charming, talented, and fun to be around. Selling Kool-Aid to pre-sweet accepting households came with its own military jargon: *launch, engagement, execute, campaigns, or my favorite, targets!* It sounded like kids playing war. Madison Avenue in all its glory."

Angie plopped down on the sofa, feeling relaxed and generous. "Weekends in New York could be lonely, so I hung out at The Factory, where Edie, Candy Darling, Ultra Violet and Nico had become my best friends. By then Andy had moved the office to Union Square West. I left their names out of my letters to Nana. Didn't want to worry her," she chuckled.

Everything changed after Valerie Solanis showed up there with a gun, pumping four shots into Andy. For a full two minutes, the hospital declared him dead. The bullets ruptured his stomach, liver, spleen and lungs, but by some miracle, Andy survived. He wore a surgical corset to support his ravaged organs for the rest of his life.

A fixture on the underground social scene, Solanis had authored a series of radical texts. Her latest, *The S.C.U.M. Manifesto*, stood for 'the society for cutting up men." In a moment of sheer madness, she'd targeted Andy, convinced he'd disparaged her script 'Up Your Ass' and stolen her S.C.U.M. manuscript.

After the shooting, The Factory lost its free-for-all spirit. Warhol installed security cameras, and implemented a strict entry policy. He turned his attention to *Interview* magazine and his artwork took on a commercial edge. The shooting marked a loss of innocence in the art world. The creative dynamism of the 1960s turned cautiously commercial by the 1970s. "We didn't know about crack or

AIDS then," Angie said. "But they were coming to ravage the city."

The news that Edie Sedgwick had died in her sleep at 28 of 'probable acute barbiturate intoxication,' came in November 1971. She'd drop by The Factory sporadically, but she'd become increasingly unstable. Finally, she left New York and landed in the psych ward of the Santa Barbara Cottage Hospital, where she met a fellow patient and married him.

Brief periods of sobriety came and went as she completed the film "Ciao! Manhattan." But mental illness ran deep in Edie's family. She'd been in and out of treatment centers, and her two older brothers, Bobby and Minty, had died in their early twenties, one in a motorcycle wreck, the other, a suicide.

Edie had as hand in saving Angie's life. If only she could have saved Edie's.

If he wasn't headed to Maggie's after work, Christian would hail a cab downtown to Café a Go-Go or the Village Vanguard to catch unknown bands that captured his curiosity. An uptown interloper in his hopsack blazer and blue oxford shirt, the bars' regulars eyed Christian with suspicion at first. But it wasn't long before they connected the dots. "Blazer guy" was a human musical barometer. Whenever he turned up, the night's band was sure to knock their socks off.

"Research," he'd call it, carefully pocketing cover charges to submit with his monthly expense reports. He'd caught the Jefferson Airplane playing in beer-soaked bars, long before they'd taken off. Christian's keen ear placed him at the crucible of an emerging 'sixties sound.' He could pick the hit single before the artist had an inkling. Today's unknown anthem was tomorrow's catchy jingle, he had learned.

Christian's passion for music inspired one of advertising's legendary coups when The Archies' single, 'Sugar, Sugar' set his imagination ablaze. *What if he could plaster a peel-and-play single of the song right on the back of a cereal box?* His young team loved the idea and set about crafting a lively client presentation.

One month later, he stood at the head of a conference table facing a trio of stone-faced executives from General Foods. "They're called 'flexi records,'" Christian began, launching into the pitch. "The Everly Brothers did one with 'All I Have to Do is Dream' back in 1960. The technology is proven. It's just another way to get good music in listeners' hands. It's going to be a huge hit. You're gonna have to trust me."

The senior client coughed uncomfortably then furrowed his brow, as if he'd stumbled into the wrong meeting. The other two clients noticed and followed suit, crossing their arms over their chests to signal their disapproval.

"Did you *read* the brief, Mr. deGraaf?" the senior client asked. "Our message is focused on moms. We want to assure them that Post cereals contain the recommended daily requirements of vitamins and minerals."

"A complete snore," Christian countered. "We're not talking about All-Bran. This is a kid's cereal. Let's be honest about that. Put a record on the box and they'll eat it up."

The junior team member cleared his throat and sat straight up in his chair. "Our buyer is a pre-sweet accepting mom who needs that reassurance," he said, citing internal research with the singular goal of impressing his boss.

"And who exactly is influencing those pre-sweet moms?" Christian countered. "Who's hanging on the grocery cart, whining for them to buy the coolest cereal on the shelf?" The younger suit's smile faded.

Christian paused to glance at his watch, a wordless gesture that telegraphed his disdain for corporate groupthink. The move worked like a charm on the creative luddites. "When you were a kid," he continued. "Did you give a moment's thought to your daily requirement of vitamins and minerals? Or, did you ask your mom to buy the cereal your friends liked?" He stopped to let this fundamental logic sink in. When the silence shifted from awkward to painfully awkward, Christian knew he'd won.

Still, the senior client wasn't ready to concede without throwing a glance at the others. "My daughter talks about The Archies all the time," the associate product manager piped in.

"Mine too," said the third client, relieved to find a risk-free point to weigh in on. With a pregnant wife and two young kids at home, groundbreaking creative innovation wasn't topping his list of priorities. He just needed to keep his job.

"I've heard the song," the second suit conceded. "My niece seems to like it. She's 12. Well within our consumer demographic."

Weeks prior the client meeting, Christian had quietly negotiated the rights to mass-produce a laminate peel-and-play single of the song. He produced a manila folder and placed it on the conference table. "Here are all the contractual details. Pretty straightforward."

"Well, *Christian*, if you think cardboard records will work," the marketing director conceded, "then 'Sugar, Sugar' it is. I have to admit you always do your homework."

"Wise decision you won't regret," Christian said. "Your children will love it and you'll sell a million boxes. Some brand managers can be close-minded. But not this Post team. You gentlemen have the creative insight to recognize innovative ideas that resonate with your consumer." He held up one hand, a televangelist performing a healing. "But you go one step beyond that," he added. "You have the forethought and intelligence to embrace a *big idea*. Now that is a rare thing, indeed. Congratulations, gentlemen."

After smiles and handshakes all around, the clients left, convinced they'd pitched the idea themselves. And when flexi-records appeared on boxes of Post Super Sugar Crisp that summer, the cereal flew off the grocery shelves as 'Sugar, Sugar' raced up the Billboard Charts to number one.

"A masterstroke," the agency's CEO gushed in the weekly update. "Congratulations to Mr. deGraaf and his dedicated account and creative team. Big ideas move products that make our clients' cash registers ring."

Who needs law school when you can send a kid's cereal *and* a hit song into the cultural stratosphere?"

Ten

After his cereal coup, Christian entered the rare air of advertising legends, his name whispered among the likes of David Ogilvy, Bill Bernbach, Mary Lawrence and Leo Burnett. Even *National Geographic* took notice, inserting flexi records of humpback whale songs into 10 million copies of the magazine.

To celebrate, he boarded a Braniff flight to San Francisco, bound for the Monterey Pop Festival. He was keen to hear the Bronx-born songwriting phenom, Laura Nyro. By the time she was 19, Nyro had written four blockbuster singles. 'Wedding Bell Blues,' 'Eli's Comin'', 'And When I Die' and 'Stoned Soul Picnic' were flooding the radio waves as Blood, Sweat and Tears, Three Dog Night, the Fifth Dimension, even Barbra Streisand scored hits by this shooting star.

The stewardess took a shine to him after he complemented her stylish uniform, slipping him bottles of vodka and Bloody Mary mix whenever she passed his empty row near the back of the plane. The uniform was all part of Braniff's bold campaign, 'The End of the Plain Plane.' To make the point, Braniff painted their jets in outlandish colors and ran ads touting the *right plane to the left coast*, featuring Andy Warhol and boxer Sonny Liston.

San Francisco recalled a younger, cleaner Manhattan, bursting with civic pride and fabulous sunsets. Californians were blonder, dressed better, and stood up straighter than the average New Yorker. Christian checked into The Fairmont, eager for a drink, and put in a call to Freddy Field, his first cousin on his mother's side who lived down in Carmel. They'd grown up going to Mackinac Island together, sharing first Marlboros and shots of I.W. Harper, while their unconcerned parents threw back martinis on the deep porches facing Lake Huron.

Freddy was an assistant golf pro at Cypress Point. Freddy had grown up in Chicago and dropped out of college to take a crack at the pro tour. But after an 18th place showing at the Clambake at Pebble Beach, he'd returned to the golf shop, playing for high stakes with visitors to the Monterey Peninsula. Like Christian, Freddy did what he wanted, because he could.

"I'll drive down tomorrow morning and we can go to this great concert at the Monterey Fairgrounds. Fantastic lineup. You can get off of work, can't you?"

"Probably," Freddy answered. "We can make that decision in the morning. Frankly I'd rather show you around this magnificent countryside in my new little sports car. See you around eleven?"

"Welcome to FeBe's. What can I get you?" The bartender, shirtless, took Christian's breath away. Patrons entering the Mission District spot on Folsom Street were greeted by a life-sized reproduction of Michelangelo's David, leaving no doubt about what they were getting into.

"How about a double Dewar's on the rocks?" The barman nodded and turned to reveal his cute, toned fanny peeking out of full leather, hand-tooled chaps. Christian reveled in the anonymity of laid-back San Francisco. In New York, he had to be discrete; here, nobody cared what flipped your switch.

"Spanking? Only $25." The girl wore a latex unitard and carried a paddle. She pointed to the stage, looking bored.

"I don't think so," Christian answered. "But I'll paddle you for free, if you'd like." She turned on her heel, as the bartender delivered the big brown scotch.

"Best answer I've heard in a long time," he said with a wink. "I'm Shane. Where are you from?"

"Christian. I'm out here from New York for the music festival down in Monterey."

"Pretty good lineup, I hear," Shane answered. "Wish I could get off this weekend." Christian turned on his stool to take in the crowd. A pretty girl outfitted in leather bondage gear lay spread-eagled over a large black wooden X, as a bearded guy in a leather hood cracked the whip. Her weak yelps and growls fell flat, taking the drama out of the scene.

Christian stood to find the men's room, passing couples making out along the dark beer-soaked hallway as 'Light My Fire' played on the tinny sound system. Christian opened the door and was startled to find an older naked man crouched like a gargoyle, next to the urinal.

The man looked to be his father's age. He wore a shiny studded dog collar and wool beanie emblazoned with a Y. "Kind young man, would you mind using me instead of this urinal?" Christian wondered if he and his father might have overlapped at Yale. Best not to ask, he decided.

A chain bound him to the urinal. Clean shaven, white hair neatly combed, the little man had once been handsome. He peered up at Christian with a hopeful grin. Shaken, Christian backed out of the men's room as the old man began singing at the top of his lungs.

When the sons of Eli
Break through the line
That is the sign we hail
Bulldog! Bulldog!
Bow, wow, wow
Eli Yale!

Nearly midnight, west coast time, the glass of big brown now seemed overwhelming. "Check please," he asked the bartender. "I'm out of gas."

Laura Nyro's jazzy, pop soul was both familiar and completely fresh. A studio musician at heart, her precision didn't translate to an open fairground of 7000 people.

Although she was only 20, her stage presence could only be described as Jewish-frumpy. Her long red nails, black dress, and masses of long dark hair were out of synch with the bell-bottoms, ponchos, and flower power style of the crowd.

She left the stage after fifteen minutes. One critic described her as 'a dreadfully pretentious woman offering up exactly the sort of formulaic pop-music piffle we had expected to avoid by gathering at Monterey." Backstage, as her agent Artie Mogull berated her, Michelle Phillips intervened, bundling the singer into her limo, where she lit up a huge joint, cracked a couple of beers, and drove around the peninsula for a half hour to shake off the moment. During this detour, soul singer Otis Redding took the stage to play the most exciting set of the night.

"It was like a crucifixion," Nyro said later. "It was like the essence of failure. And I believe in great failure and great success. I don't like anything in the middle. I learned that I was a formidable musician, but I had to get my shit together."

Christian had been talking up Nyro for weeks, but Freddy had a different plan in mind. "I know your heart's set on seeing that girl sing," he announced when Christian arrived at his place in Carmel. "But I've got the whole day off," he said. "And I'm not spending it at a crowded fairground with a bunch of dirty hippies. I have a friend who has a vineyard about two hours into the mountains. It'll be far more civilized. Trust me. I'll call him right now."

They sat down to a magic mushroom omelet before Freddy bundled Christian into the passenger seat of his Alfa Romeo. "Wine country," he said, slamming the door for emphasis. "I'm driving." A decade ago, after a brief stay at Smithers, Freddy gave up the Beefeaters, turning his attention to wine.

As Nyro took the stage in Monterrey, Christian found himself 75 miles into the mountains near Soledad. The mushrooms had erased any peevishness he might have felt about missing her performance. "Get this," Freddy says as they headed southeast towards the mountains, "I have been doing research on vineyards in the area. The climate out here is better than France. California will be the center of wine-making in a decade. Mark my words."

They'd been driving wild-eyed for nearly two hours into the Gavilan Mountains, when neat rows of grape vines came into view. Freddy downshifted before turning onto a steep gravel driveway along the rugged slope of Chalone Peak.

As the Alfa labored up the final stretch of the hill, Christian turned to take in the view. A tanned hunk of a man sat astride a tractor, shirtless, plowing the field ahead. At the sight of the car, the man flashed a bright smile and waved. *Breathtaking view,* Christian thought. Dickie Thomas was a vision, an Apollo in cut-off fatigues, tending to his land. "What have we here?" Christian said, rubbing his chin, mood lifting.

"I told you, that's Dickie who just started this vineyard. I wanted you to meet him," Freddy teased. "But hey, if that hippie concert looks better to you, I'll turn this car around …"

"Not necessary," Christian said, "given that fine looking piece of machinery up ahead." He slipped a furtive glance at his cousin. "I think you've made your point."

"Here comes trouble," Dickie yelled, stopping the tractor near the spot where Freddy had parked. "What are you on today? I've seen those wild eyes before. And what on earth are you driving?" He climbed down from the tractor and offered a firm handshake. "I would have met you with the truck if you told me you were coming. I do have a telephone now." Dickie looked over at his guests shaking his head. "You know this road isn't suited to little Italian sports cars and city drivers? I'm amazed you actually made it. But you're here and just in time for lunch and my newest release, a pinot noir."

Dickie Thomas had majored in music at Harvard before travelling to Tibet to study Zen Buddhism with the Dalai Lama. After his father cut him off, he changed course and enlisted in the military where he trained as a naval aviator. For two years, he lived on an aircraft carrier in the Mediterranean. After that, he decided to set his sights on making wine.

When Thomas bought the remote mountain property, it had little to recommend it beyond an old chicken coop, which stood amid the scrub brush in a state of disrepair. The place lacked water, electricity, even telephone lines. Undeterred, Thomas announced plans to turn the place into a French-style winery. "Dickie has a way of making things hard on himself," Freddy noted.

With money borrowed from his mother, he started planting grapes high in the Pinnacles National Park, then hired a local winemaker. He released his first vintage last year. Christian noticed he sat ramrod straight on the tractor, the impeccable posture of a Navy pilot. Dickie still made more money selling mistletoe and Christmas trees than wine.

Thomas was a man of mystery who originally lived in the Haight after his military service. His family was originally from Chicago and he'd gotten to know Freddy's parents during summers up on Lake Huron. He was alternately formal and irreverent, now living alone in the mountains. There were rumors he was dishonorably discharged, but nothing was ever that clear about his military career. He still kept a Cessna down the mountain at Paicines.

After four bottles of wine, the conversation turned to Viet Nam. Thomas had been stationed on the USS Alameda County in Souda Bay in Crete during the late fifties. He didn't like what he saw coming in the French colony of Vietnam and resigned his commission after one tour. "Can't get involved in these civil wars, particularly the Asian ones. Korea was a waste of lives. You'd think we'd learned our lesson. Look at us now. What a waste! And LBJ is doubling down. Stupid rube."

"Why are we throwing young American men into the middle of a faraway war again? This is crazy. How's it gonna end?" Men of privilege, like Christian, Dickie and Freddie, could find ways around the draft if they desired. This war would be fought by poor whites, Negros, and a few patriotic believers. The American soldiers would find themselves on the ground, in hot, wet, snake-infested jungles where booby traps lay concealed under thick elephant grass. If you were smart, you would learn to fly a helicopter, but that didn't guarantee you wouldn't come home in a box. The pictures on TV looked awful. Christian considered himself a conscientious objector and a scaredy-cat to boot.

He tried every trick in the book to avoid the new draft. Christian was a little old at 28, but you could never be sure. His father assured him that a career in law would allow a permanent deferral, implying the flaky ad industry offered far less protection. Johnson had escalated the war over the past two years, arguing about 'falling dominoes.' The pictures on TV were horrific, the heat unbearable.

Dickie Thomas had served his country; he earned his pacifist stance. But his military bearing, crew cut, and fit figure suggested otherwise. They bantered about music, too. Dickie, like Christian wanted to go to Monterey, but he couldn't get away during planting season.

"Hey, if you get a chance," he told Christian as the afternoon wore on. "Check out this guy named Jerry Garcia. They play all around here. He's got the perfect name for his band, look 'em up. They go by the Grateful Dead."

Eleven

Nobody knew Christian better than Duella Graves. She'd come to work for the deGraafs when he was a baby, and never left. A part time pastor in the Greater Bethel African Methodist Episcopal Church on West 123rd Street, she was the granddaughter of Elizabeth City North Carolina sharecroppers. But to Christian, Duella was his best friend.

As a boy, he went everywhere with her, including Sunday services at her Harlem church. His parents thought it was splendid that their curious boy was exposed to the world beyond the cloistered Upper East Side. Duella's son Clinton was a frequent guest at the deGraafs. The two of them drew occasional stares from neighbors and suppressed smiles from doormen, but Marge was determined to raise her son to be the right kind of snob.

Harlem was Duella's true calling. She advocated for her neighborhood, calling herself as a 'community activist.' She used her time with the deGraafs to bring them – and their world into her causes. It was only fair.

So far, New York had been spared the riots that gripped Newark across the river, but Duella's finger was on

Harlem's pulse. "Just a tiny match could blow the whole city to smithereens," she told Marge. "Lindsay needs to do something for the Negros in this city." She took a sip of sweetened ice tea and continued. "You know what would keep the pressure valves open this summer? How about a concert in Harlem showcasing Negro music?"

Marge relayed Duella's idea for a concert to Christian, who did some research before mentioning it to Isaac over cocktails one evening. "Think of it, father, she's got a point. Why do the white kids get a concert up in the Catskills? A concert in Harlem celebrating Negros and their music is way overdue. I've checked into it. We could get Count Basie, Tito Puente, and Mahalia Jackson. Plus, some of the new soul singers like Gladys Knight, Stevie Wonder, and the Staple Singers. We can call it Harlem Hollywood Nights."

Isaac nodded. Pop music festivals weren't remotely in his wheelhouse, but Christian could be pesky when he got an idea in his craw. "We could add a fashion show, boxing demonstrations, a go-cart race, and maybe even the first Miss Harlem contest?" he continued touting. "It's a good way to keep the peace this summer." Then, ever the pitchman, he added casually, "by the way, isn't Lindsay planning to campaign for re-election soon?"

"You've got a point," Isaac said, steepling his fingers in thought. "He hasn't endeared himself to the voters of Harlem. Hell, I can't think of the last time he set foot there. Good politics. What's the price tag?"

"I have a guy named Tony Lawrence, he's a concert promoter who can put this on for peanuts," Christian said, hands dancing as he talked. "Can you imagine? The concert could pay for itself. And I've got a hunch we might find a sponsor. I've floated the idea by my client at Maxwell House. This could bring revenue to the neighborhood. Please talk to the mayor, Father. He listens to you. And you don't want to disappoint Duella, especially when she's right."

Isaac took the idea to the mayor, applying gentle pressure, calibrated precisely over days. By weeks' end, he'd worked Lindsay into a lather over the injustice. "Sullivan County puts on a big music concert, too," the mayor fumed. "Why aren't *we* doing that for Negros right here in our city?"

"Couldn't agree more," Isaac responded, the next steps nicely laid out by his son. "I think we may have a good lead on a sponsor. If we lock that down, this won't cost the city a dime."

Christian called Tony Lawrence with the news. The concert promoter and community activist directed Harlem's JFK Youth Foundation and the Christ Community Recreation Center. "Good Lord, Christian," he said in his gentle island lilt, "when I think about what the revenue from the concert could do, it's a blessing, truly. We've had our eye on a few vacant lots. Just think, if the concert raises enough money, we could buy them and convert them into small neighborhood parks. I'll make some calls, we'll get a great lineup. God bless you Christian. Thank you for calling with the news. Did you tell Duella yet?"

"Just hung up with her, Tony," Christian replied. "And she'd got a request for you …"

Tony made his next call on behalf of his friend Duella Graves. She'd asked for Count Basie specifically and Tony knew his agent. "Music's not just for young people," she'd told Christian. "We've got to get BB and Mahalia, too."

Tony met Duella in the 1950's. He'd moved to Harlem from the Caribbean, dead set on launching a career in entertainment. By 1962, Lawrence had appeared in 'Dr. No' and had a Billboard top 100 hit to his credit. She'd introduced him to Christian after church one Sunday as 'The Continental Dreamboat.' From his clothes to his cars, everything about Tony was flamboyant. Together, he and Duella were a force for Harlem.

In a bright green suit, he welcomed 300,000 people packed into Mount Morris Park, and introduced the mayor to a crowd as 'our blue-eyed soul brother' to a big roar in the crowd. Duella just smiled at this New York coalition.

Duella's son Clinton, who worked for Congressman Adam Clayton Powell, also had a hand in making the event come to life, running interference with the Parks Commissioner. Usually in city politics, everyone nods, shakes hands, and proceeds to do exactly what they want. Clinton was determined to ensure every detail – from trash pickup to stage construction, security guards and porta johns – was approved, permitted, and ready. Despite costing nothing, he'd been allocated a slice of Maxwell House funding, and he was dead set on spending it wisely.

The concert was set for Mount Morris Park on July 20, 1969, a stroke of luck. That very night, the astronauts of Apollo 11 would land on the moon at 10 p.m. Christian smiled at the possibility. "What a soundtrack! We want every TV in Harlem on with the landing, and windows wide open to the music," Christian told his father. "We'll be making history!"

"Nina singing 'I Put a Spell on You' while a man lands on the moon, all in one night?" Duella said beaming, when Christian told her about the coincidence. "That's no coincidence, honey. God's fingerprints are all over this one. That's his plan; I feel it. We are blessed, indeed, Christian."

On the big night, he sat next to Duella in the block of seats Clinton had staked out near the stage. He looked over the program, sharing it, just as they'd shared a hymnal on Sundays. Stevie Wonder, Gladys Knight, BB King, Nina Simone. The stars were aligned at City Hall, everything had fallen into place. "This really is Duella's doing," Christian told Clinton as he sat down in his lawn chair. "This is her Woodstock!"

Nina Simone kicked off the concert at 7:30. Duella had known her for a decade and they shared the same values around civil rights. While Duella just wanted to open minds and to broaden the prosperity tent to the next generation, Nina used her talents to protest far more loudly and sharply. She recorded her hit 'Mississippi Goddamn' in 1964 after Medgar Evans was murdered.

In a particularly wonderful moment, Mahalia Jackson, the granddaughter of slaves, like Duella, invited a young

Mavis Staples to join her for a duet. A hush fell over the crowd as their voices mingled in a transcendent rendition of 'Precious Lord, Take My Hand,' Martin Luther King's favorite song. When Christian glanced at Duella, her eyes were fixed on the stage as silent tears ran down her cheeks.

Sly Stone came out for the final set dressed in fuzzy boots, a gold necklace, and a rhinestone-rimmed cowboy hat. "That's one *crazy*-looking nigga," Duella said, laughing as she ribbed Christian and pointed to the stage. "What on earth does that boy have on? Lord, we're a long way from Jerry Butler, bless his soul." A space age electric horseman, Sly was part Elvis, part Little Richard, and all Sly. His spaceship band echoed his music; half white, half black, part female. Sly had a magnetic way about him, making people point and smile. But his music held a message for the thousands assembled in Mount Morris Park that night, and they were listening:

There is a yellow one that won't
Accept the black one
That won't accept the red one
That won't accept the white one
Different strokes for different folks
And so on and so on and
Scooby-dooby-dooby

The humidity dipped for a few hours on that July night, as if on cue. Duella Graves sat back in her lawn chair sipping her soda, marveling at this rare and magical moment, suspended in time and forever solidified in her memory. And as Sly worked the stage, thousands of New

Yorkers jumped to their feet, hands in the air, singing 'Everyday People.'

Twelve

Clara emerged from the kitchen with a fresh bottle of wine and a corkscrew. "New York was fun back then," Angie said as she offered up wine from the freshly uncorked bottle. "The mood was upbeat. We had the Jets and Mets, two world championship teams. I'd even found a few allies at the agency. I became friends with Toni, who worked with Norman Brighton, the other creative director."

A bow tied English gentleman, Norman was no fan of Steve Caputo. "Why would anyone wish they were an Oscar Mayer Wiener?" he asked Toni once, when his door was closed. Still, he accepted the American consumer with their fickle sensibilities. Norman brought a twinkle of mischief to his role, along with impeccable manners. Widely respected within the agency, Norman's reputation extended to Toni, who could type nearly 100 words a minute. After fifteen years with the agency, she was the unofficial den mother of the admin staff.

Toni could spot a bull shitter. She'd grown up with Steve's type. She knew Sicilians, too. Steve wasn't from Bergamo in the north as he claimed. That was obvious. "He gets away with this crap because no one dares to cross him," she told Angie in the breakroom, a few weeks after she started.

Toni craned her neck, looking for anyone within earshot. "Just do your job," she whispered, taking a sip of coffee. "Keep work *separate,* You're not friends, remember that." Then she opened her purse and freshened her lipstick in the mirror of her compact. "Chin up, doll. If he *looks* at you wrong, you come to me." She capped the tube, closed the compact, and dropped them back into her purse, snapping it shut. "Got that? I'm onto him, Now let's get back to it."

"When Steve asked me to dinner to celebrate my six-month anniversary, I didn't think it was separate from work," Angie said, rolling her eyes at her own naivete. "I was picturing a big steak and an Idaho potato, dessert if Steve was feeling generous. Who was I to argue when he suggested I reserve a table at the Four Seasons on Sunday night?

"By then I'd found a tiny one-bedroom in the East Village. After groceries and rent -- $285 a month was a lot of money back then – I could barely swing dinner at the Chinese place on Mott Street. Beyond work and The Factory, I didn't have a social life to mix with work. But I remember that evening like it was yesterday.

"Good evening, Mr. Caputo," the maître d greeted us. "How nice to welcome you again tonight. You always have such attractive guests," he said, nodding to me. "Follow me, please."

"As soon as I walked into that shining space, all glass and steel, full of old rich people, I felt underdressed."

"This is New York's most famous restaurant," I remember Steve whispering, leaning close as we crossed the room to a corner table. "President Kennedy ate here whenever he came to the city in the fifties."

"I was in awe and felt important among the movers and shakers of new York City. Truthfully, I was checking for celebrities. Compared to Horn & Hardart, I'd stepped into a dream, or a movie. I'd never seen so many waiters and busboys, *platoons* of small men in white jackers bustling about in silence among the large tables, all spaced around the calming pool at the center of the room. Except for the occasional clink of silverware, there was a hush over the dining room, like a church. It was like I was in a dream."

I remember Steve smiling at the maître d', gesturing toward me once we were seated. "William, this is my assistant. We're celebrating Angela's six-month anniversary at Y&R" he said, following with, "Angela? What would you like to drink?"

"I'd like a Beefeater gin martini, please," I replied confidently. Mind you, I'd never had a martini before, but it sounded sophisticated, like the thing to order. When the maître d' smiled and said 'excellent,' I felt like I'd passed the first test."

'And William,' Steve said, clearing his throat. 'I'd like a double Jack Daniels and Coca-Cola, please. And I'd like to reserve a Grand Marnier soufflé for dessert.' He turned to me, "Their soufflé is to die for; a toast to your fine work."

"I looked around the room, excited. Here I was at the Four Seasons having dinner with one of New York's best-known ad men, a regular who's on a first-name basis with the waitstaff. Not bad for a girl who'd stepped off a bus with $905 in her pocket, not knowing a soul. Steve had been a good boss so far, a perfect gentleman. He was rewarding me for good work."

May tapped her pencil on her chin. "What on *earth* did you talk about?"

"Idaho," Angie laughed. "He asked me about the LDS church, what it meant to grow up in that world. Polygamy. That always comes up first," she continued, glancing at Clara. "With that subject out of the way, he asked about my family, fly fishing, and the Rocky Mountains. I told him about Reggie playing ball there, watching him from the bleachers in Lewiston before he moved up to the majors. When I mentioned I'd worked for Andy at the Factory, Steve sat up in his chair. I couldn't place exactly why, but the question definitely had a predatory feel to it."

"You know Andy Warhol?" he asked sharply.

"Well, sort of," I answered. "When I first got to New York, I met a girl who invited me to stop by and check it out. The cinematographer hired me on the spot. They would have hired anyone, I think. I worked mostly for Billy, but Andy was always around. Nice man, definitely odd. Hard to believe someone tried to kill him."

"I read that," Steve said. "When you get too famous, crazy people want to kill you."

"*Crazy people?* Want to *kill you?* I was taken aback. Words were Steve's stock and trade; he didn't make off-key remarks by accident. He was testing me, I think. Looking for a reaction.

"William returned with the drinks, gently placing my martini on the table, my own little sculpture. We toasted to future success. That first sip tasted harsh, but cold. I took a quick belt and felt the icy fire go down my throat. Martinis must be an acquired taste. I relaxed a bit, taking in the oversized windows. Instead of curtains, aluminum chains rippled against the bronze mullions, creating the illusion of a steady golden rainfall. If the place needed a hostess, I would have worked for free, happily."

"Another martini?" the waiter asked, pausing at the sight of my empty glass.

"Yes, thank you," I answered happily. "I wanted dinner to last all night. The first one had gone down quickly, leaving me a sunny twinkle. I was easing into this urbane setting. I belonged there too, after all. I was Steve's guest."

"We talked through the salad course, three mint-infused lamb chops, two glasses of Bordeaux and the soufflé – I remember how it tasted to this day. Sublime. Meanwhile, Steve's still asking about Andy Warhol.

"I can't say we've sat down for a chat," I told him. "But I mean, he's talked to me, mostly about lighting or props. I help with his movies on weekends. He just did a weird one called 'Blue Movie.' I worked on that one."

"Sounds risqué?"

"It kinda was. Andy said it was about the Vietnam War and how love wins over destruction." She turned to May and Clara with a facepalm. "Already, I'd said too much. The whole 140-minute film featured a couple having sex in a New York apartment. Plot and dialogue were never high on Andy's list of artistic priorities."

Steve leaned in, intrigued. By now, the martini was talking. "Most of Andy's movies are about sexual disappointment and frustration," I said, hoping to tie the topic into a tidy bow and move on. "He sees the world the way nine-tenths of people see it, but pretends they don't."

"At this point, I didn't really want to go much further. The plot centered on a couple having sex in a New York apartment and it lasted 140 minutes. The dialogue and plot were minimal.

"Are you sexually frustrated?" he asked, intrigued by the notion of this all-American girl from 'out west' working for Andy Warhol.

"I'd stepped over the line, thanks to the gin. So I resolved to slow down. Change the subject,' Angie recalled, shaking her head.

"No," I said, hoping to shift gears, distract him. "So, tell me about your children …?"

He looked up, with a short smile. "I'd rather talk about you."

Thirteen

When the Grand Marnier soufflé arrived, Steve ordered a nightcap before Angie could object. "Two sambucas, please," he told the waiter, who nodded and disappeared. "Tell me more about yourself. What an interesting life!"

Angie looked to May and Clara for encouragement. "I had led the conversation into a stupid place and wanted to start over. But it felt thrilling to talk about sex. Where I grew up, drinking coffee was scandalous. Then I remembered Toni's advice. "That's personal, Steve," I told him. "We're here to talk about work, remember?"

"I don't recall leaving the restaurant, or how I got home. But I woke up with a raging headache. I didn't dare open my eyes, thinking, 'please God, don't let this be the Roosevelt.' If I'd gone to his hotel room, then I must have done something to encourage him."

May and Clara looked at each other, then back at Angie, dumbfounded. Clara had never heard this part of Angie's story. She knew Steve was a pig, but now she wanted to hunt him down herself. It broke her heart to hear Angie blame herself for what happened.

"The hard part was going to work the next morning, trying to keep my concentration and focus. He'd ordered up breakfast in bed for us, but I was mad at myself. It's such a cliché to sleep with your boss. I was better than that. I needed to write Nana, but maybe leave out a few details of my new and interesting life as a New York ad girl and a minor role in a racy Andy Warhol movie."

"So, let me get this straight," Clara used sarcasm to make her point. "*You're* the one who invented the tired cliché of sleeping with the boss? And you think you encouraged *him*? He's got a wife and children for *Chrissakes,* Angie. You're not the temptress who lured him into sin. Give me a flipping break."

May was squinting at the ceiling, doing the math. "Tell me – I mean, not for the profile – but *how old* were you at this dinner? Twenty-one? Twenty-two?" She flipped through her notebook searching for the reference. "And remind me Mrs. deGra … I mean Angie. How old was Steve?"

Clara was angry now. "That guy is a master manipulator. He knew what he was doing when he dreamed up that ridiculous excuse for a dinner. Six months on the job? A celebration dinner? At the Four Seasons? Are you *kidding* me? And remind me again?" she said. "Which one of you was the *creative director*? Do you see the power differential there?"

"I guess … I mean yes. I know. I guess you're right," Angie stammered. The generational gulf around sexual abuse was staring back at her in May and Clara's faces. Why was *she* still making light, blaming herself all these years later? "I was smart. I was talented. I was better than that. I knew it. And he knew it, absolutely. The hardest part was going to work the next day."

"I wish I could remember leaving the Four Seasons. But after he ordered a second Sambuca, all bets were off. Steve was a gentleman, I guess…"

"Angie!? *What the absolute fuck?*" Clara was angry now. "*What are you saying?* Think about this, right now, look at me—what kind of gentleman gets his assistant drunk, then date-rapes her while his wife is home in Teaneck tucking their children into bed? What part of this are you not seeing?"

"Well, I guess…" Angie wasn't sure. "I mean, he ordered breakfast in bed for us. And when I went into the bathroom to take a shower, I noticed a condom wrapper in the trash. I was so mad at myself. The hardest part was going to work that day."

May put up a hand, signaling a pause. Then she leaned forward, taking Angie's hand in both of hers, looking her in the eye. "You did nothing wrong," she said softly. "Can you hear what Clara is telling you? She's right. You did nothing to encourage that. Nothing."

"I guess so," Angie said. "Thank you, May. I did have a sort-of boyfriend at the time. It's not like I was loose." She covered her face with her hands, confused by the shame bubbling from deep within her after so many years. "When I opened my eyes in that dark smelly hotel room, I just knew I'd screwed up big time."

Angie steadied herself, forcing a smile and checking her watch. "It's almost ten, ladies. Can you keep your eyes open for another half-hour? Now that we've dug into that old wound, we might as well finish it off."

May smiled. Angie had assumed the role of chronicler. May liked her self-deprecating style. The rock stars she'd interviewed so far had cloudy memories at best and rarely strayed from hagiography. Her last ones, with Robert Plant and Jimmy Page, made little sense once she'd transcribed the tapes, despite the list of questions she'd submitted to their agent in advance. Compared to the Led Zeppelin piece, Angie's story would be a piece of cake. She'd already begun toying with a few ideas for the opening.

"Tell us about the Andy Warhol movie that got you in trouble?" Clara urged. "It's nothing to be ashamed of. Certainly not after all these years. Like everything else, it was silly and harmless ... until it wasn't."

"Well, my sort-of boyfriend worked at the Factory, too. He went by the name Jack Dakota and he fancied himself a performance artist, even though he was a stage hand, like me. Andy never paid attention to job titles, so people made them up sometimes. Jack was trying to break into acting but I couldn't see the talent, even though he was gangly and cute in a slight, undernourished way.

"Jack was always happy to help out. We had been sleeping together over the past year or so, although I suspect he preferred men. My sex life is a whole other conversation, as you've discovered tonight," she tried to laugh, but caught herself. She didn't want to disappoint her young guests.

104

"One of our sexcapades wound up in Andy's film, 'Spa Boy,' about a handsome guy who serviced the female guests at a health club. When the actor Andy had cast in the title role came down with a stomach bug, Jack was drafted as his understudy. And, since I was *already* sleeping with Jack, they handed me the role of Tiffany Danger, the pampered heiress looking for forbidden romance in, I guess, a health club?" she chuckled at the absurd premise.

"Without little direction, we stripped off our clothes and climbed onto a massage table where we tried to perform sixty-nine without falling off the thing. Jack wasn't used to the idea of other people watching—the whole *lights, camera, action* thing. The scene lasted maybe fifteen minutes with a lot of starting and stopping. I was already sleeping with Jack, so I didn't think much of it," Angie said. "Showing my naked body to the world? Who cared? I could have sex whenever, wherever I wanted. That was freedom. But looking back now, I don't know what got into me, besides terrible judgment."

Angela Lovejoy's job description now included satisfying Steve Caputo sexual urges, which often consumed her lunch hour. "Still, I was booking his Sunday night table at the Four Seasons. By then, the maitre'd and I were on a first-name basis. He'd give me the receipts to type up his expenss reports, including the Roosevelt Hotel tabs, all listed under 'client entertainment.' The whole situation was humiliating. Was this how a woman built a career?"

"God, no," Clara could hardly contain herself.

Deflowered by Jared Bingham, coerced by Steve Caputo, Angie wondsered whether sex was worth all the trouble when a single night could bring a lifetime of pain. Jack was sympathetic. He never took advantage of her. But he was busy having sex with other men. She wondered what normalloving sex was like. Maybe someday, she'd find out.

When a job in TV production opened at the agency, she asked Steve to promote her. She'd learned film production at the Factory. She knew the job; soliciting bids from directors and producers for TV commercials, getting clients to sign off on estimates, writing call reports, booking talent, keeping everyone happy. She already did some of it as a secretary. Occasionally, she'd meet someone semi-famous. She was more than qualified.

"He promised to put in a good word for me, but nothing ever came of it," Angie said. "Turns out he was lying. I talked to Toni about it, multiple times."

Steve Caputo belonged in jail, Toni insisted. Instead, they handed him the Merrill Lynch account.

The brokerage house had approached the agency with one question: How could Merrill Lynch stand out from the others, namely, Paine Webber, Dean Witter, and E.F. Hutton? They all peddled the same blue-chip stocks and bonds and their names had become interchangeable. "Are you telling me," Steve asked in the first client meeting, "that the best Merrill Lynch can come up with is 'We Look for Trends'? People come to you to make money, not for lifestyle advice. What use is a trend anyway? The term is imprecise and abstract. No one cares. It's a wasted opportunity."

The marketing manager had commissioned a customer research study. "Based on our data, customers are looking for a knowledgeable financial provider to help shape their financial future," he replied. The six meeting attendees smiled and glanced at one another, to see if anyone could make sense of this lightly-dressed word salad.

Steve bit his lip and sized up the group assembled around the table. A bunch of lightweight MBAs, he concluded. "It's too wishy-washy. Tentative. Your clients want something strong and bold. You're an industry leader, not a fashion coordinator."

The senior client nodded uncomfortably at Steve's assessment. "We like to think of ourselves as the leader in providing customized financial solutions to our clients." He sat back, assured that his clarification would straighten the brand strategy question.

Steve leaned forward, bringing his hands together as if in prayer, nodding. The account team looked alarmed. They were hoping their creative director's comments would garner a polite response, but they feared the worst. "I believe your vision is good," Steve lied convincingly. "But what exactly is a customized financial solution? The words feel dense and squishy. Let's boil this down. Merrill Lynch sells the stock market as a place to put your money. To make money. Let's keep it simple."

"But we want to tell clients that we're their financial advisor who can ensure long-term financial success," the client answered, grasping for words. "We provide a total solution."

Steve smiled quickly, wondering how this meathead had gotten so lost in the world of business jargon. "How about this?" Steve began slowly, looking out at the room like they were a cohort of six-year-olds. "For centuries, financial markets have used the terms 'bull' and 'bear.' Let's start with the bear, since, according to Merriam-Webster, this mascot of market sell-offs emerged first." Steve scanned the room slowly, making sure he looked at each of the clients in the eye.

"The term is derived from "bearskin" which was used in the 18th century as a metaphor for speculative stock buying. It comes from a proverb that cautions us not to 'sell a bear's skin before one has caught the bear." The senior client's smile was frozen in place. He was trying to figure out where this yarn was going.

"The idea," Steve continued, "is that a bear attacks by swiping its paws *downward* on its prey. A downward swipe means stocks will go down. A bull, on the other hand, thrusts its horns *upward* to gore the poor souls who cross its path. The upward thrust means stocks go up."

Steve was keeping a close eye on reactions to his economic history lesson, as he turned over a foam core board, with a dramatic flair. "It's very simple, ladies and gentlemen: Merrill Lynch is bullish on America." He paused, noting the senior client's smile, still fixed in place.

"I envision a barren western landscape," he intoned dramatically. "From across the plain comes the far-off thunder of thousands of hoofs charging towards the camera right onto Wall Street." Steve paused, looking directly at the senior client. "Merrill Lynch equals a perpetual bull market." He stopped right before the punchline, almost daring the others in the room to take him on, enunciating slowly. "Ladies and gentlemen, Merrill Lynch is bullish on America."

The client's market research analyst jumped in, interrupting Steve's reverie. "We can't *say* that. Stocks go up and down. Everyone knows that. We can't promise a bull market." The designated downbeat client voice, required in every agency meeting since the dawn of time, her name was Karen. She wore thick glasses beneath her blond bangs and silk blouse tied with a bow at the neck. She insisted she represented the 'the voice of the consumer'.

"We're not promising anything, but I understand your concern," Steve answered gently. He had to shut her down gracefully. He'd watched brilliant pitches get derailed when the research lady piped up. "Bullish means optimistic. It's very American." Steve knew patriotic references always win the day and he wasn't going to be taken down by this plain Jane. He looked around the room to size up the other reactions. "After all, Merrill Lynch is a breed apart," he tossed in breezily. "We're not the other guys." The heads finally began to nod in unison.

The senior client liked Steve's response, blowing off his cautious colleague. "Do you think we can find a herd of bulls to film running along Wall Street?" he laughed. "We can own strength and optimism too. I love it!" Steve was on a roll. He imagined a herd of fifty bulls running through Lower Manhattan. It a big idea that would further burnish his reputation, securing his position above the rules.

Steve could already script the *Ad Age* and *Wall Street Journal* interviews: How did *you* come up with such an iconic idea? Why are *you* so bullish about America? Have you looked around at this decaying country? New York is hardly a shining city on the hill anymore. And, who's going to get rid of all the bullshit? He could already see the gag commercial with all of Wall Street ankle deep in cow pies.

Still high on himself, Steve summoned Angie into his office later that afternoon. She walked past his shelf full of hardware and sculpted glass tributes, taking a seat in front of his desk. "Why don't we have a little rendezvous to celebrate our success at selling bullshit?" he winked. "A great day for the team."

"Can't today, Steve," Angie said, glancing at her watch, trying her best to sound matter of fact. "I've got a meeting across town and I'm running a little late." Angie hadn't had time to look for another job, but she had to get out of this mess. Steve would never promote her. All he cared about was lying on top of her for five minutes, then he'd send her on her way to clean up his mess. That much was clear. Her life was going sideways.

"What kind of meeting?" he asked.

"It's personal, Steve. Just like I said at the Four Seasons, remember?"

"You're not interviewing. Are you? If you're going out to an interview, just tell me. I'll write you a letter of recommendation. You're the best secretary I've ever had." Then his face clouded as he shifted gears. "We're a team, Angie, a damn good team whose work makes our clients' cash registers ring."

"So I've heard," she responded. "You've fed me that line five times in the last month. Then, when I'm up for a promotion, you block me."

"Not true," he retorted. "It's just that I can't afford to lose you."

"Well, Steve," she said, standing up to put on her coat. "You can't afford to *keep me*, either. Now, if you'll excuse me, please, I have to be somewhere. Congratulations on Merrill Lynch. Brilliant presentation. See you in the morning."

She'd bought herself an uneasy truce. But three weeks later, Steve summoned Angie to his office and asked her to shut the door. "I've been nosing around about Andy Warhol. I think he might be a good spokesman for a new client, Chanel. They want something new and edgy."

Angie smiled. "That's great, Steve. If you like, I'd be happy to mention it."

"No, that's OK," he answered flatly. "It's just an idea in the incubator. Always gotta have a bunch of them." He smiled quickly.

"Anything else?" she asked. He was acting weird.

"Yeah," Steve said. "I saw one of his movies last weekend: 'Spa Boy?' Heard of it?"

Angie's cheeks flushed red as her stomach fluttered. Was Steve desperate enough to resort to blackmail? Her mouth went dry. "Yes," she said, trying to sound casual. "I remember 'Spa Boy.' Just a fun thing I did with my boyfriend one weekend."

Steve tightened the noose. "Maybe *we* could do a little sixty-nine next time? What are you doing this afternoon? Sex with a porno star sounds exciting."

"I don't think so. Steve, I'm not comfortable with this conversation."

"Well, you're clearly comfortable in the sack. I'd bet you could teach me a thing or two. I'm just an old guy from New Jersey. Your john."

"Your *john?* What's really going on here, Steve?" With nothing left to lose, a calm settled over her, rooted in a deep rage. "Keeping me on the hook with your promises? How many promotions have you torpedoed? You know damn well I'm qualified for the production job."

"Who the hell do you think you're talking to?"

She looked him up and down in his silly custom shirt. "Hard to tell, Steve. Dr. Zhivago? Look, I don't need this. I'm out," she barked, getting up from her chair, voice quivering, hands shaking, heart pounding.

"You *can't* leave," he snarled. "You wouldn't dare. I'll tell everyone at this agency that you are a porno star. I'm sure your grandmother will love that news. This is Page 6 of *The Post* material: *Mormon girl trades life of purity for sexual debauchery and sex for hire.* You like that?"

Angie sat stunned at his words, feeling her world collapse. If her famous boss exposed her, no one would listen to a porn actress crying about sexual harassment. She couldn't stay, but she couldn't afford to quit, either. Angie always spoke the truth and, in that moment, something in her snapped.

"Steve, you are a shameless predator and I'm not subjecting myself to this for another minute. Remember, I do your expense reports, so I *know* you're a liar and a cheat. You'll get your comeuppance. But I won't be here to see that." She'd seen this story before. Men abusing women without conscience and fear of retribution. What could a secretary do to a powerful creative icon? It was part of his compensation package.

"Be gone, then," Steve barked, flicking his hand toward the door as Angie gathered her purse and the small framed picture of Nana she kept on her desk. "Go on back to the land of the weirdos. I'll have someone in the talent department call Warhol's agent. He did those Braniff and Burger King ads so we know he's for sale, just like you."

Fourteen

"Whitney's been asking about you, Christian," Marge was on the phone, working herself up to her patented full-court press. "We've got box seats, no small feat I might add. And big surprise, your father can't make it so I've got the extra ticket for you. Martha Gerry's coming. And when was the last time you saw Ogden?"

He wasn't much of an equestrian fan, but Christian agreed to meet Marge in Elmont for the Belmont Stakes. The box seats came courtesy of Whitney Tower. Her old friend and Saratoga Springs journalist was covering the race for *Sports Illustrated*. Christian enjoyed the pomp and pageantry of horse racing, but mostly he enjoyed dressing up, socializing, and daytime drinking. Marge was right. The gang was all there. Ogden Phipps, Martha Gerry, Joan Payson, Nick Brady, assorted Harrimans. But today was about Secretariat, poised to make history.

The railbirds and drunks had filled the stands to the rafters, racing forms clutched in their sweaty hands, torn tickets strewn on the floor. Even Marge had been known to get a snoot full at Belmont Park and place bets based on nothing more than the color of the jockey's snappy silks.

Penny Chenery sat several rows down in the owner's box, looking calm as ever. He'd met her at parties in New York over the years and admired how well she had managed the horse, already being compared to 'Man of War' as the greatest racehorse in history. Large Marge liked seeing a woman was in charge. "What an inspiration! A woman with horse-sense. This country needs more Penny Chenery's!"

Marge looked happy in her straw hat, sipping a generous glass of Chablis. The late spring afternoon prompted Osborn Elliot, *Newsweek's* editor to crack, "It's a nice break from Watergate to the starting gate." Everybody had become a horse racing fan over the past six weeks, and today they were hoping to witness history.

Although he was the overwhelming favorite, Secretariat faced the stiffest test of the Triple Crown at the 105th Belmont Stakes. Several horses over the years had won the Derby and the Preakness, only to falter on Belmont's mile-and-a-half track. Most lacked the stamina to run this punishing distance. Those that did, were often weakened by the Derby and the Preakness that preceded it, all in the past month. The short recovery time meant that anything could happen; injury, fatigue, rider error, weather, and luck -- all converging to tip the outcome. The excitement surrounding this race had sent fans into a frenzy, with dreams of hitting the big payout.

Steve Cady of the *New York Times* wrote that Secretariat could be defeated if the pace of the race went too fast or, conversely, remained slow for too long. In either case, he believed the contender, Sham, was too good a horse not to win one of the three races. Sham had received significant attention and was thought to be the second-best horse, along with having the potential of becoming the first horse to be runner-up in all three Triple Crown races.

At 5:38 on that muggy afternoon, 70,000 spectators and fifteen million viewers watched as Secretariat broke sharply from the five-horse pack. There would be no lazy beginning, no stalking from behind, or leisurely acceleration this time. He took the rail immediately with Sham on the outside. After one furlong, Sham had the lead by a half-length but Secretariat stayed with him, gradually passing him at the half-mile post. With a half mile to go, Secretariat, unhurried by Turcott, plowed ahead to build on his lead and simply galloped away from the field. His only competition was himself.

Christian noticed Secretariat's coat change color as he ran, turning from light brown to auburn, then to a deep chestnut as fibrous muscle in his body churned like the pistons on a diesel engine. His hooves hit the track so fast that his white-stockinged legs moved in a blur, like a vapor trail. The blazing pace, the ever-widening margin, the rhythmic drum beats of hooves, and the horse's breath, calm and steady, would remain a moment forever frozen for jockey Ron Turcott, sitting chilly, glancing over his shoulder.

The horse and rider were all alone, moving as one. Twenty-eight lengths, now thirty-one. They crossed the wire in two minutes and twenty seconds, a new track record. Christian had just witnessed the most stunning moment in horse racing history. No other horse had come close. When Secretariat died in 1989, his autopsy revealed that his heart weighed more than twice that of the average thoroughbred. 18 pounds, compared to 8.5 pounds typically.

Angie sat in her dark, stifling apartment watching the race on her tiny black and white TV. Her living area consisted of a reclaimed sofa she found on First Avenue, and eight milk crates that supported a wood veneer door that served as her dining table. Chairs were a mixed bag of acquisitions. Her life in a nutshell. But watching that horse run away from the field made her happy that she was witnessing history and greatness not far from here. Her life was anything but. She was tired of being broke, irritable, and drenched with sweat.

This summer had been particularly miserable and she longed for Idaho's dry mountain air. Window fans were useless, blowing dirty hot air from the street. Everyone on her block was half-dressed and irritable. She couldn't even afford a cheap air conditioner for her tiny apartment on East Fourth Street off the Bowery, compounding her crankiness.

After nearly four years of menial work at Y&R, Angie was shaken by her sudden departure. If she'd known the job was a dead-end, contrived to satisfy her rapacious boss, she would have left sooner. But Steve's promises of a promotion while demanding sexual favors had left her demoralized. How could anyone be that cruel and selfish?

Angie's sex life was off to a bumpy start. It started with being raped by an older family friend, then devolved into a series of on-demand booty calls from her boss. Only her relationship with Jack America was rooted in affection and desire, but he preferred men to Angie. Love was out there somewhere, but so far it was illusive.

She had gotten a few commercial acting assignments through friends at Y&R over the past few years. Her slender build, pretty plain face and ample blond hair made her a natural for the new Clairol Herbal Essence Shampoo ad campaign that began running on TV in March. She laughed that here she was again, being filmed up close with limited clothes on, this time in a shower and not a bathtub. At least she would be paid the SAG rate.

Angie picked up a few other assignments, but they were unpredictable and few and far between. A lot of people in New York were trying to break into acting. Over the past year, Angie played a young mother with three kids in a Jell-O commercial that aired over the summer. The residuals amounted to a few thousand dollars, not remotely enough to make rent or eat out.

Angie needed to get a new job or get really lucky with more commercial or acting work. All she thought about was work and money and how she craved both. A steady office job was tempting, but she didn't want to go back and become dependent on someone else again, particularly a man. Angie had decided to pursue acting and modeling. She finally realized it was why she came to New York. Angie kept up with Y&R friends and met regularly for drinks at Maggie's Bar on 48th Street.

Angie's looks were wholesome, her attitude scrappy and people wanted her to be successful. She had another casting call next week for a young mother in a Post children's cereal ad. She had to memorize a few lines about the nutritional value of Fruity Pebbles ('As a mom, it's important to buy cereals my kids will eat, knowing they are getting a healthy daily dose of vitamins to make them strong.')

She wondered about the ingredients in the box of Fruity Pebbles that she was praising, but no one seemed to be concerned about it. Angie worked hard and stayed busy, but she was still broke, just on the edge of making it to the bottom rung. Ramen noodles and slices of pizza would have to do it for a while longer.

Later in the summer, Jack and Angie landed roles as extras in 'The Great Gatsby.' They got to dress up in tweed suits and flapper dresses and stand around a huge party with forty others, looking and acting swell. It wasn't the breakout part either had been hoping for the past four years, but at least it was paid work and they got to meet Mia Farrow and Robert Redford. Jack lived a few blocks away in a tiny studio off Avenue A and they pooled resources from time to time when they needed to.

They were occasional lovers and looked after each other, but Angie could tell that Jack preferred men. He would disappear for a few weeks and sometimes come back with a black eye or bruises. They saw each other every few weeks, sharing late night drinks and sex if the mood was right. Mostly they talked about upcoming auditions, while bemoaning their feeble finances. At 27, she was too old to ask Ada for help. But she felt like she was paddling in the middle of a dark ocean, looking for something firm to grab onto.

July 25, 1973

Dear Nana:

Things continue to go well in New York, although I quit my job last week. I've told you about Steve, my boss. He was nice at first, promising to help me get promoted. Turns out, he was lying. I really want to be a producer; you know the person in charge of making TV commercials for the agency? But now he says he can't afford to lose me. So, I guess I should be flattered?

I've started going to auditions, to see if I can do some acting. I got a call next week as an extra for 'The Great Gatsby'; they're filming the movie here. I'm hoping I'll get to see Robert Redford. What a dreamboat! And I get to wear a flapper dress! Beside that job, a friend from the agency is keeping an eye out for modeling work.

Don't worry. I'll be just fine. I'll keep you posted.

Love, Angie

Fifteen

As soon as he spotted the tiny, classified ad in the *Village Voice,* Jack called Angie. "Listen to this one," he said when she answered. "Now casting for a major motion picture," it read. "Tryouts 4 p.m., Wed. 10/21, 1973." The address listed was a few blocks from his apartment, but the ad didn't mention the movie's title. "Might be sketchy. What do you think?"

"Sounds iffy," she told Jack. "That feels off."

In the year since the Steve Caputo debacle, she'd picked up a few acting gigs through her Y&R allies, thanks to Toni. They'd meet for drinks at Maggie's Bar on 48th Street every other Thursday. Angie's wholesome looks and scrappy survival skills worked in her favor.

Her latest TV ad, for Clairol Herbal Essence Shampoo, began airing in March. Instead of a Lucite tub, she was filmed in a shower for that one. For a Jell-O commercial, she'd played the mother of three young kids. But the few thousand dollars she earned in residuals were not remotely enough to make rent. New York was a magnet for aspiring actors. The competition was fierce. She needed a job, or a steady stream of commercial work.

She'd been memorizing her lines for next week's Fruity Pebbles casting all when Jack called. The client, Post cereal, was obsessing about the cereal's nutritional value: *As a mom, it's important to buy cereals my kids will eat...* the script read. The technicolored flakes were clearly loaded with dyes and preservatives. Angie figured the agency copywriter needed the paycheck almost as desperately as she did.

"What kind of 'major motion picture' holds a casting call on Avenue A, of all places? Gatsby was filmed in a proper studio. But who are we to be picky? If they're paying the SAG rate, we should give it a look."

Their best job so far had been 'Gatsby.' They were cast as extras for a party scene, dressing in tweed suits and flapper dresses along with forty others faux guests. Everyone looked swell, but the extra's job is to blend in, rather than stand out. Still, they got to meet Mia Farrow and Robert Redford during filming; and for two days' work, the pay wasn't bad.

Jack's studio apartment was off Avenue A, just a few blocks from Angie's. They looked out for each other, pooling resources, comparing notes on auditions, and meeting occasionally for a late-night drink to bemoan their feeble finances. When the mood struck, they'd have sex. Their friendship was rooted in affection and seasoned with desire. She didn't think of him as her boyfriend.

It wasn't that simple to define. Jack would disappear, often for weeks at a time, returning with bruises, or a black eye on occasion. Given a choice, Angie figured Jack preferred men. Still, it felt good to have him in her corner.

Love had long eluded her but, with Jack, she'd begun to believe it might be out there somewhere, within reach.

They were right about the classified ad. The 'studio' was on Fourteenth Street, next to a funeral parlor, in a dirty basement apartment. The casting director, a long-haired hippy in overalls, stood back, sizing them up. "I'll need pictures," he said abruptly, motioning for the photographer. They stood against a white scrim for several shots, both together and apart.

Next, he asked Angie to remove her shirt and bra. "The movie has a few nude scenes," he said matter-of-factly, skipping the question of whether this might be an issue. "Our producers want to see the actors in a realistic context. It's just part of the casting process," he said casually. "Have either of you done any nude modeling before?"

Jack looked at Angie, alarmed. "As a matter of fact, we have," she said, summoning the last scrap of confidence she had left. "We did a movie for Andy Warhol a few years ago called 'Spa Boy.'"

The photographer sat up from the rusty folding metal chair. "Warhol, wow! All right, then. Good. You get it," he replied. "Do you work exclusively with one another?"

"Yes," Angie jumped in, nodding toward Jack. "We're a package deal. What's your rate?"

"A hundred-and-seventy-five bucks each. Full day. That's our high end," he answered. "Let's shoot some

Polaroids and see how you look. If they're good, I'll call you. We're filming on the Upper East Side. *Classy* production. We can make an eight-millimeter loop."

On the walk home, Jack was quiet. "Does Andy's stuff count as a porno movie? It's so weird, who would ever get aroused watching it?"

"Who knows? Who cares? I already lost my job over that stupid movie," she said. "I'm broke. Shampoo and cereal ads aren't cutting it. Shame is a luxury I can't afford right now. I need the job, so I'm in. But if you're feeling squirrely about it, don't do it for me."

Jack laughed. "I'm not sure my parents in St. Paul will see it that way. Neil Simon and Carol Burnett are more their speed. But I'm an actor, sort of, and we're already having sex. So what difference does a camera make?"

"My grandmother warned me about New York's temptations," Angie continued. "You know the bite from the Big Apple? But I have to admit that filming that silly Warhol movie with all of our friends was the most fun I've had in this city. Hell, we only go around once! Anyone who pays money to masturbate while watching us have sex on that loop has bigger problems than we do." This made Jack laugh. "And heck, we're just a couple of broke actors. Maybe we could do an instructional video .... for beginners?

"Yeah, you're right, although I'm sure I'll regret it," Jack said, throwing an arm around her shoulder. "I have a confession. I've only had sex with one other girl besides you. I'm still trying to figure it out."

Angie paused, looking over at May and Clara, for clues. The embarrassment lingered after all these years. "I knew that this decision would stick with me for the rest of my life. There is certainly shame in doing a porno movie, although I was numb about it at the time. I was broke and needed the money. It wasn't a big deal. Everyone has sex, but only a few don't mind others watching your performance. I remember thinking, 'let's just get on with it.'"

"We took a taxi to an apartment on the Upper East Side, just off York Avenue in the 80's, not far from Gracie Mansion. It was an anonymous fifteen-floor residential high-rise on a monochromatic block. It instantly brought back memories of The Factory and getting my first job in New York City. I'd never forget taking that creaking, smelly, banged-up service elevator to that dirty floor with spotlights, weird people, and silver paint everywhere.

"The elevator bell chimed as we reached the eighth floor. I looked ahead along the non-descript dingy hallway with a beaten-up sisal runner along the floor. 'It's not too late to back out,' I remember saying to Jack. "Last chance."

"I just spent my last dollar on cab fare. Can't turn back now," Jack said, giving her a playful squeeze."

A willowy girl, barefoot and wearing a sarong, answered the door to #8D and introduced herself as Lia, the film's production coordinator. She showed them around the set, introducing them to two men tending to the lights and camera. The film's director, Vito, was short with a big smile, but said little.

Angie suddenly had second thoughts. 'Spa Boy' may have been a porno movie – they did have sex on screen – but it was also an Andy Warhol film -- experimental, artsy, but certainly not indecent. Was there a distinction? She knew this would be her scarlet letter, but what would it matter? *Go for it, girl.*

Vito insisted 'Young Starlets' was a film. "First of all, it's about real people, just like you," he struck a semi-serious tone, "young, ambitious New Yorkers." This one would be different, a series of vignettes about the real-life challenges of a successful talent agent and Angie, you are a song-and-dance girl from Lima, Ohio who wants to make it big."

From the looks of the dingy bedroom, filled with rattan furniture and bright polyester fabrics, nobody was making it big yet. The Levitz chairs were slipcovered in drab corduroy, the headboard a shock of orange velour, was trimmed in large buttons. The apartment looked like a Southern California bordello. Lia took the pair into the kitchenette to sign release forms. "One question for you, what are your stage names?"

Angie laughed, "Hadn't thought about that." She paused. "Well, I'm Angie and my last name is Truelove, so how's 'Angela True'?"

"Don't you want something more anonymous? Might be better long term? It's a little like getting a tattoo," Lia answered with a crinkled nose and a wry smile.

"Nah, I like my name," she answered. "That's all I got. You know, sleeping in the bed you made, so to speak?"

Jack jumped in. "I'll go with Jack Dakota. It's already my stage name. My real name is Stan Wachowski."

"You never told me, Stanley," Angie roared. "Good move. I like Jack Dakota better."

The conversation relaxed the pair and Lia showed them to a second bedroom to change. "Just be yourselves and hang loose. Do you want a joint?"

"Sure," Jack said. "Anything to get us in the mood. We're not used to performing on command."

"Do you need 'fluffing?'" Lia asked. "You know," she motioned with her left hand clenched, rotating up and down.

Angie looked up and laughed. "I think I can manage that part."

'Young Starlets' became a hit in the winter of 1973, joining 'Black Heat,' 'Finishing School', 'Honey Buns', and 'John Holmes Fuck-o-Rama' in the top grossing films of the year. *Screw* Magazine called Angela True 'a gift to the industry' with a 'feline build, honey-colored hair, flawless peach skin, upturned nose and downturned mouth.'

No amount of flattery could beat a paycheck. For the first time in eight years, Angie had some money. "Young Starlets' grossed nearly $20,000 and brought stacks of requests from casting directors. Vito immediately lined Angie up for three upcoming movies he was directing over the next two months. He also volunteered to be her agent.

For each movie, 'Angela Love' would receive $2,500, which specified two scenes and new partners. Her luck had turned. She'd tried being a secretary, a production assistant, a model, and a commercial actress. Now that she'd become a porno star, she'd tapped into a steady source of income. Sex and love had long been separate for Angie, but still she preferred the familiarity of shooting scenes with Jack. When they performed together, he never needed fluffing.

September 1973

Dear Nana:

Before you get all excited, it's a small role, not even a speaking part, but I won out over fifteen girls. I'm the new Clairol Herbal Essence Girl! It's not like I can quit acting, but at least I can pay my rent and go out to dinner occasionally. Modeling and acting are tough to crack, but I'm getting there slowly. It's like the Frank Sinatra song, 'if I can make it here, I can make it anywhere.'

I have a boyfriend named Stanley, but he likes to be called 'Jack.' I can't blame him. He's from Minnesota and wants to be an actor too. He's very sweet and protective and we like doing the same things. I've met a few new people in the music business too.

I'll write next week. Angie

Angie smiled as she read the letter out loud. "I may have neglected to tell my grandmother the whole truth during this period. I did go to every audition I could find for *anybody* who was hiring models or actors. I had no choice."

"Nana knew something was up," Clara corrected her. "She read me that letter a few years later with raised eyebrows. Nana didn't know exactly the details of what you were doing to support yourself, but she sensed that you weren't completely forthright in that letter."

Angie made a face. "I did an awful lot of rationalizing back then."

Sixteen

"Porn paid the bills, like any job." Angie put a log on the fire. The room smelled of cedar and pine. "I found a better apartment. I bought an air conditioner. I could eat in a restaurant without worrying whether the check would bounce. That's when I started going to hear new bands at CBGBs, which led to my first moment on stage."

The first time Angie took the stage, it was with The Velvet Underground. "I got called up to join them. I'd met Lou Reed and John Cale at The Factory years ago. Back then, they played at Max's Kansas City, the house band," Angie said. "I had a half-assed stage presence, and I could handle back-up harmonies. I'd had no formal voice training, unless you count sixth-grade choir practice." She shot a knowing glance at Clara, who'd been booted from the same choir. "If acting wasn't happening, why not try pop music?"

Angie kept in touch with Toni at Y&R. *"Everyone* knows he's an asshole," she told Angie, nearly in tears. "But no one dares to call him out." Steve's behavior reflected the basic laws of physics. As his creative skills ascended, his morals plummeted, in equal-but-opposite proportions. "And you won't believe this, Angie: The agency just *handed him* the Quaker Oats account, for God's sake." Angie felt lucky to be out of there. Getting fired was a blessing.

"I've talked to HR," Toni said. "I've told them none of my girls feel safe around him. They pat my hand, sympathize, and do absolutely nothing. I keep thinking he'll hit rock bottom but, with Steve, there is no bottom. The man is sick."

From the moment it launched, Quaker Oats' Life cereal was dead on arrival. Although the plain brown woven hexagons were loaded with sugar, the cereal lacked a personality or spokes-character like Sugar Bear or Snap, Crackle, and Pop; leaving little impression on shoppers.

The clients flew in from Quaker headquarters in Minneapolis, betting on Steve Caputo to save their brand. After a few pleasantries, the six of them took seats around the conference table and turned expectantly to their creative savior.

"Let's start with the box," Steve began, swiveling gently in his chair, gazing upward in thought. "You've got a pudgy old man wearing a bouffant wig. He looks like my creepy uncle," Steve wasn't holding back. "Then you open it, and the cereal itself looks like pine mulch."

Everyone in the room froze. The Y&R account supervisor began mentally writing the apology letter he'd need when the client called seething: *How* dare *you insult the Quaker Man?*

Then, as if he'd taken a Quaalude, Steve softened, mustering a smile. "I rarely find inspiration at home," he said dreamily, as if he'd found the key to a divine portal. "But Life cereal had *given* me that opportunity. My neighbor in Teaneck has a finicky four-year old named Mikey. He's the youngest of four brothers."

Steve looked around the table, searching for buy-in. "I trust several of you have kids of your own," he said nodding, as most of them nodded back. "So you know this already: no kid will try something new if their parents are pushing it." More nods, a few smiles. "Right? They double down until it becomes a test of wills. And at that point, you can fuhgettaboutit." More knowing chuckles, some at Steve's expense.

"So how does the *gatekeeper*, the mom who's making the purchase decisions, integrate Life cereal into her own family's mornings?" Steve let the question hang in the air, a subtle tease. "The *parents* can't do it," another pause brought a few confused frowns. "That's when it takes *kid mastery*." He placed hand to heart, invoking his own boys, Rocco and Tony. "For my children, Life cereal is the sweet fuel they happily eat before school each morning," he fibbed. "But it took a *dare*, from one brother to the other, to get those boys to try it."

Quaker's senior client had three blond children back home in Minneapolis. She was hanging on Steve's every word. "Imagine this," he whispered, meeting her eyes. "Two kids eye a bowl of cereal with suspicion. Kid 1 asks,

'What's this stuff?' Kid 2 replies, 'Some cereal. Supposed to be good for you.' Kid 1: 'Did you *try* it?' Back to Kid 2. 'I'm not gonna try it, you try it.' Kid 1 slides the bowl to Kid 2. The bowl slides from the first kid to the other, but neither one is willing to try it. Then Kid 2 hits on a brilliant solution: 'Let's get Mikey!' Kid 1 remains skeptical. "He won't eat it. He hates everything …'

The room erupted in laughter, so Steve set up for the big finish. "Mikey grabs the spoon and digs in, as the other brothers sit up and take note. 'He likes it!' Steve exclaims in his best kid voice. By now, the senior client has tears in her eyes. Steve delivers the kicker, adopting a subdued voiceover: "When you bring Life home, don't tell the kids it's one of those *nutritional* cereals you've been trying to get them to eat. You're the *only* one who has to know…. Camera fades to black." Steve had taken to tossing in a bit of moviemaking parlance, a final flourish. He had them, even before picky Mikey showed up.

As the accolades poured in, Toni became even more enraged. "It's so bad that personnel, I mean *human resources*, won't even interview new hires for him. So now, this *shithead* is hitting on the temps!" Toni paused to collect herself. "Angie, somebody needs to take this man down."

"If I did nothing else in New York, I was determined to stop Steve Caputo from hurting anyone else," Angie told Clara and May. "I called my friend Candy Barre. A sexy firecracker, Candy was always up for taking down the bad guy. Candy and I bonded on the set of 'Darling Debutantes II.' We both threatened to walk when the producer added anal sex scenes to the script, *after* we'd signed contracts, based on the original script," Angie said with a chuckle. "Even porn stars have standards." Clara laughed, May winced.

"Candy and I stayed in touch. I remember her talking about Linda Lovelace 'making it big,' with 'Deep Throat' in 1972," Angie said. "That movie grossed over $600 million. Guess what *Linda's* cut was? $1,250. Her work grossed hundreds of millions of dollars and they gave her the scraps. Her husband was a monster, beating her black and blue, making her do weird shit like dog and piss movies. It's a demeaning business. We needed out."

"Let's go out to New Jersey and confront him, in front of his wife and kids," Candy urged. "We should do it publicly, maybe at one of his kid's football games? We'll humiliate him on his home turf," She nodded to herself excitedly. "How about we dress up as hookers? Tease our hair all big and slutty? He'd love that."

Candy's eyes got big, She had an idea. "I've got a four-year-old nephew! We can bring him along. We'll call him Little Stevie. He'll be the 'love child' you've been raising alone." She had more: "And now you're confronting him to beg for child-support, so that his son won't have to be put into foster care, and you can quit porn and hooking." She was pleased to see how their takedown was unfolding.

"It's all a show for his wife," she continued, her voice gaining momentum. "I know these types, Angela. We'll have fun with this, hamming it up and taking him down at the same time. This son-of-a-bitch has been cheating—on his wife, his mistresses, and abusing his secretaries his entire life. Time for Mr. Caputo to face the music." Angie liked Candy's chutzpah. There were no half-measures with this girl.

They rented a baby-shit brown Vega sedan from Avis for the hour-long trek to Teaneck, hometown of The Isley Brothers. During the drive, they talked about how they'd fallen into the adult movie business, lamenting how it had lost its quirky homemade style. "It's always been a little shameful, but now that there's a huge audience, so it's all business. Directors want more, more, more sex to film," Candy laughed. "It's a lousy way to make a living. But hey, it's legal."

'Little Stevie' sat in the back seat, staring out the window, happy to spend the day with his aunt, with the promise of five dollars and ice cream, afterward. "Honey, you'll be great," she reassured him. "Don't be afraid to hug him around the knees. The mothers will love it."

"Men really suck," Candy said, then turned to the back seat, "except *you* honey! You'll grow up respecting women, right?" The Vega sputtered off I-95 at the Fort Lee exit, headed for Hawthorne Elementary School, just as the community league football game was starting.

As the two women wobbled across the damp field in spiked heels, holding a cute little boy by the hand, they drew stares. "Let's make sure the mothers see us," Candy directed. "The dads will notice before we're out of the car. Horny Jersey boys can't help themselves."

Angie waved as she approached Steve and Carmen. "Honey! It's me! Remember?" She'd never met Carmen in person. Short, a little dumpy, with frizzy dark hair, she wore brown square sunglasses and bright pink lipstick.

"And Little Stevie?" Candy's nephew extended his hand. Steve looked confused, sweat beading on his forehead.

"Hi Pops," the nephew said, on cue.

The look on Steve Caputo's face was worth this wacky stunt. Particularly after Little Stevie ran up to 'Dad' and hugged him around the legs, squeezing with astonishing credibility, as the fans in the bleachers *oohed* and *aahed* at this adorable father-'son' reunion. This was getting interesting.

"Do I know you?" Steve asked, staring straight at me.

"Course ya do, Stevie," I answered in my loudest Brooklyn accent. "We used to fuck like rabbits at the Roosevelt Hotel. After ya' Four Seasons Sunday night *client* dinners? You love Grand Marnier soufflés and Sambuca. Then you fired me when I told 'ya I got pregnant with little Stevie."

Angie had managed to work up a few tears. Candy had coached her on a proper Brooklyn Italian accent. "*Drop your 'r's'. Then change ya th's to d's.*" The word 'those' sounds like 'doze.' Angie pulled it off: "I *daught* we were in love. We *tawked* about running away to Taormina. I'd be ya' full-time muse and love slave."

"I been out on my own since. It's *hawd* raisin' our boy alone," I continued. "He asks about his *fawtha* all the dime. I just thought ya' should meet him, ya' know, before we set up visitation and all."

Steve's infidelities were no surprise to Carmen. In her world, men would be men. But a public reveal? A boy clinging to his leg? That was unforgivable, a betrayal of the family. Steve's excuses about working late and client dinners now made sense. "Is this true, Booby?" she asked firmly. "Are these your whores? And that's your boy? He looks like 'ya. Explain, please." Her stubby hand, glowing with hot pink nail polish went to her hip, indignant.

Carmen Caputo was not to be fucked with. She may have been frumpy and hardly noticeable, but her maiden name DeCavalcante demanded respect. Her father Sam owned Kenilworth Heating and Plumbing, gaining the nickname 'Sam the Plumber.' The last thing that Steve needed at this moment was involving him in the marital affairs of his only daughter. Sam had just finished serving five years for racketeering and now lived in a high-rise condo in Naples, Florida. His reach remained extensive in the tri-state area.

Carmen knew Angela's voice; they'd spoken on the phone a few times, but Steve's assistants came and went like the wind. "I'm waiting, Steven," she stood, tapping her foot. "As is your *dawter*."

The conversation between the two 'hookers,' a cute little boy, and the Caputos, was catnip to the couple's coterie of friends and neighbors. To them, it was simple:

Steve, the bigshot ad man, got caught with his pecker outside his pocket. The douchebag was in big trouble. Rarely did anything this exciting happen on a Saturday morning at Hawthorne Elementary. "She's making it all up," Steve pleaded. "I wouldn't do that to you honey. You know me."

"I know you're a low-life philanderer," Carmen clapped back, loudly. "But when you're spreading your seed all over town, we got bigger issues booby. What the hell is wrong with you, ya fucking dumbass moron?" His daughter Lucia appeared just then, back from playing on the swings with friends. "You want to explain this to your *dawter*? She's old enough to understand adultery."

Seventeen

Once the *New York Post* made hay of Steve Caputo's epic infidelities, he became a tabloid piñata. 'Icarus and the Wings of Man: The Fall of America's Philandering Ad Man' read one *Daily News* headline. The *Post* countered with 'Oscar Mayer's Wiener, Unzipped.' Even the Teaneck *Daily Voice* piled on, sourcing 'reputable Y&R insiders' for their own salacious stories. As the ink spilled, readers figured Steve must had boinked every other woman in the tri-state area.

Each woman's story was strikingly similar, exposing his modus operandi: Dinner at the Four Seasons, cocktails, wine, Sambucas, the Roosevelt Hotel, and condoms. When it came to sex, Madison Avenue's most brilliant creative director displayed a stunning lack of imagination.

Dismissed from Young & Rubicam and booted from his home, Steve sublet a one-bedroom apartment near Lincoln Center. The six-month lease, he reasoned, would give him time to restore his tattered reputation and find another job.

But a toxic predator is a tough hire. The big agencies wouldn't touch him. His calls went unanswered; his messages, unreturned; his letters, unopened. If his award-winning resume did land on a hiring manager's desk, it was promptly filed under: 'How about *never*? Is *never* good for you?'

Even God was fed up with Steve's bullshit, throwing a thunderbolt, sapping him of his creative powers. When a small direct-mail agency let him go after a month, the great Steve Caputo finally hit rock bottom.

Like every scorned Sicilian woman, Carmen Caputo was not to be crossed, particularly in public. She'd hired a part-time private detective to keep tabs on her wayward husband. But after three months, the detective called her, defeated. "I can't keep taking your money, Mrs. C," he said, finally. "Your husband has not left his apartment in three weeks, possibly four. If his door opens at all, it's to tip the delivery guy."

Phase One completed, Carmen issued an ultimatum to her so-called husband: "If you *evah* hope to set foot in ya house again, I'll need *proof* that my booby is a changed man. Don't even *dink* of coming back until you can be the husband and *fawtha* me the boys deserve."

With nowhere to turn, Steve Caputo requested a brochure from Eberhard Seminars Training, known as 'est.' He'd heard the term tossed around at the agency; now est was turning up in magazine articles and on morning talk shows. When the brochure arrived in the mail, the testimonials echoed variations on a theme: *"It changed my life."*

Celebrities, from Yoko Ono to Valerie Harper extolled the virtues of est. But the seminar itself was impenetrable: *Beings begin as pure space or context and manifest themselves through content.* Steve read this sentence twice. This unintelligible mixture of random words served on a four-color gatefold of heavy cardstock with a matte finish was his only hope.

The following Saturday morning, Steve stood among two hundred and fifty people at the Marriott Midtown waiting for the ballroom doors to open. At the registration desk, one of the half-dozen chipper volunteers checked his name off a master list, confirming payment in the amount of $250. Once cleared, the clean-cut young man handed him a white name tag which swung from a black lanyard. "You're all set!" he said. "Wear this during the seminar, at all times." The nametag read simply: Steve.

No longer Steve Caputo—the maestro of Madison Avenue, Four Seasons regular, wrangler of hotshot clients, fashion iconoclast, and creator of iconic ad campaigns. For the next two weekends, he was simply Steve, stripped of rank, title, custom shirts, even his own last name. *Like a toddler entering nursery school, I am Steve*, a thought he found mildly amusing.

Once the doors opened, he chose an aisle seat in the ballroom. The straight-backed chairs, arranged in ruler-straight rows, were divided into three sections, and angled toward the stage. Trainers patrolled the perimeter, enforcing a sacred silence. At 8:30 a.m., sharp, the lights went up, and a dour man in an argyle sweater stepped on stage, introducing himself as Rick. The warmup act, Rick opened a thick binder and, without preamble or so much as a smile, launched into the seminar's draconian rules.

Sessions would begin each morning at 9 a.m. No late entries. Each day included a single 90-minute meal break. Sessions could last until midnight. No talking. No leaving the room, except during prescribed breaks. No smoking. No eating. No drinking. Bathroom breaks would be staggered at intervals, in alphabetical order. For the Zachs and Zoës in the room, this news was concerning.

Note taking was strictly prohibited. Wrist watches and timepieces must be turned over to a training assistant for safekeeping until the session ended. Rick droned on for nearly two hours until, finally, a cheerful, spirited man dared to raise his hand.

Rick acknowledged him, extending his palm to signal 'hold,' while making a looping gesture with his other signaling a training assistant to scurry down the aisle. Rick directed the man to stand, while the trainer handed him a microphone. Only then, did Rick say: "Question?"

"Yes, I have a question," the man said. "Why all the rules?"

"Because *Werner* found out what *works*," Rick said. The man furrowed his brow and sat down as the room erupted in applause, another *est* mandate.

Steve bristled at the forced discomfort, the rigid protocols, and the weird cultish vibe permeating the ballroom. *Why were they being treated like military school truants?* Steve wanted transformation, and *est* defined that tantalizing promise in wispy, vaporous terms. He *needed* it, whatever it was, to get his life back. If it meant forking over $250 and sitting for hours over two tedious weekends, he was willing to give it a shot. But his patience was already fraying.

At 10:30 a.m. sharp, Werner Erhard bounded onto the stage, microphone in hand. Fit and angular with coiffed dark hair, he looked like a middle-aged Alpine athlete, strong but graceful. "In this training, you're going to learn you've been *acting like assholes!*" he shouted. "All of your fucking cleverness and self-deception have gotten you *nowhere*."

'*Okay*,' Steve smiled, recognizing himself. He sat up in his chair. Not too long ago, Steve Caputo insulted his own paying audiences. Now, that he was simply 'Steve,' he'd be getting a taste of his own medicine. Erhard might have a point.

What Steve Caputo did not know was that the handsome man scowling from the stage had plucked his name, Werner Hans Erhard, from an issue of *GQ* magazine. The name had a ring to it: precise, disciplined, vaguely Austrian. It suited him better than Jack Rosenberg. Born in Philadelphia, Erhard (aka, Rosenberg), married his high-school sweetheart, fathered four children, and sold automobiles, both new and used.

Erhard (aka, Rosenberg) then abandoned his family, vanishing to marry another woman. Public assistance kept the four Rosenberg children fed and clothed. As for credentials, Rosenberg (aka Erhard), had none. He was neither certified nor trained in philosophy, mental health, motivational psychology or, for that matter, event planning. His est program was a home-brewed mashup of Zen Buddhism, cybernetics, and fascism with a dash of Dale Carnegie thrown in for good measure. Graduates of his est program often gravitated to Scientology.

Had Steve Caputo been in possession of these facts, he would have walked out of the ballroom, rules or no rules. Instead, he sat through a barrage of insults, as Erhardt berated his audience, calling them *worthless human beings*, clinging to *false truths* rooted in reason, logic, and understanding.

"Don't give me your goddamn *belief system*, you dumb *motherfucker!*" one trainer screamed at a man, who'd dared to assert that humans did possess an innate need to believe in *something*, whether God or a higher power. The trainer stood within an inch of the man's face, screaming like a pissed-off NFL coach after a Super Bowl fumble: *"Get rid of all that shit!"* Stunned, the man sat down, only to be greeted with a burst of applause.

By late afternoon, the trainers were lecturing about victimhood. "We create our own reality, from illness, to automobile accidents, to street muggings, no excuses. Anyone wishing to rebuild their life will succeed only after accepting this fact." Ever the salesman, Erhard's promise of transformation, at $250 a pop, had made him a wealthy man.

The following weekend, Erhard bounded on stage and launched into a mind-numbing three-hour lecture on the anatomy of the mind. "I'll tell you everything there is to know about life," he promised. "What is and what isn't. True enlightenment is knowing you are nothing but a collection of brain-powered machines. Whether or not you accept this as so," he paused. "It's so." The lights in the ballroom dimmed as the audience was left to sort out this bizarre message.

Steve sat in his straight-backed chair, exhausted and confused, as Erhard continued, "This is the miracle of est. You are what you are, responsible for everything you do. Each of you now are what you always wanted to be. In a word, you are perfect, just as you are."

The audience cheered, their applause punctuated by shrieks of laughter, even a few gasps. Erhard held up a hand, to silence them. "I'd like a show of hands from everyone who 'gets it.'" Dozens of hands shot up. But Erhard turned his attention to those whose hands remained by their sides.

"*I* don't get it," Erhard said, addressing a trainer across the room though his microphone.

"Good," the trainer answered. "There's nothing to get—s*o you got it!*" The exchange had the sound of a tired Vegas schtick, or a send-up of Abbott and Costello's *Who's on First?*

"I *get* it!" Erhard answered, a broad grin spreading over his face. "So getting it is—whatever you get."

"If that's what you got." The trainer bowed, as if thanking Moses for descending the mountain, tablets in hand.

It would take time for Steve to unpack the two weekends, or to know what stuck. Despite the insults, he felt better. He couldn't be sure but, somewhere over four tedious days, his mind may have shifted. Carmen would demand a blow-by-blow account of what he learned and why he deserved another chance. His mind was blank, wiped clean. Was that the point?

Eighteen

Angie stoked the pot belly stove with kindling to chase off the morning chill. They'd talked until close to midnight, but she'd always been an early riser. May wasn't due until 10 a.m.

She was on her second cup of coffee when Clara returned from the market with a basket of bagels, cream cheese, and some mixed fruit. They sat together in the cool morning sun, listening to the birds, when they heard a gentle knock. "Our journalist is prompt," Angie said, checking her watch. "It's five to ten."

"Come on in," Angie shouted as she stood to open the door. "We're having a little breakfast. Dig in. Bagels are fresh; but they can't compete with Manhattan's, coffee is over there on the table. Would you prefer tea, May? Ready for battle?"

May slashed her box of pens like a sword and smiled sheepishly. "Pens sharpened; questions locked and loaded." She enjoyed the laid-back rhythms of Angie's household, where formality was not a priority. "First, I wanted to thank you for being so open yesterday." May was growing more confident with each encounter. "Most interviews are stiff and formal, guarded, which I understand. They wind up feeling shallow. Famous people are often so guarded, afraid to be themselves."

"Well, thank goodness you're not interviewing a famous person then?" Angie shrugged with an impish grin. "So where were we?" She took a sip of coffee and peeled a banana. She was ready to go.

May checked her notebook. "You and Candy got even with Steve."

"Right. So, I'm pushing thirty with eight commercials and two movie cameos under my belt. Not exactly 'making it' by Big Apple standards. But then I got a call from my agent, Herb Klein. I hadn't heard from Herb in months, since I did a Fruity Pebbles commercial," she laughed, recalling her phony 'mom' roles.

"Herb talked like an actor in an old movie: 'Toots,' he says, 'I've got a Jamaican real estate group looking to record a commercial jingle. They want an All-American girl, so you're perfect. They'll fly you down, put you up in a nice hotel, and pay you a grand. I'd jump on this one, kiddo.'" Angie added some context. "Work was tough to come by then—I'd show up for a Shake 'n Bake casting call and find myself competing against twenty other women. So, now I'm hearing *Come to Jamaica?* I'd never left the country! I'd need a passport. I was floored."

Christian deGraaf always enjoyed a mid-winter's trip to Jamaica. His parents had been going to Half-Moon Bay since the early fifties. Isaac was among the original investors, along with Harvey Firestone and Richard Reynolds. This year, he'd brought along his friend Carlos, an actor and model he'd recently hired for a Maxwell House commercial. Young, fit and gorgeous, Carlos would be a joy to have around for the week.

Ahead of the trip, Christian had written to Federal Records owner Ken Khouri to request a tour of the Kingston recording studio, Jamaica's first. Ken had recorded Bob Marley's first single 'Judge Not' there in 1962. He'd spend the rest of the week indulging in his usual routine: waking and baking out in the morning sun, then moving a hundred feet to the beach to order a silly drink to sip while reading 'Tinker Tailor Soldier Spy.'

Ken invited him to drop by anytime. A local ad agency had booked the studio that week. An American pop singer would be there recording tracks for a real estate ad. She'd be done by noon by the latest.

Housed in a modest yellow building on Hope Road, Federal Records had expanded over fifteen years and now included a mastering and stamping room, cassette pressing plant, wholesale record shop, and a booking agency. Photos of Marley, Peter Tosh and Jimmy Cliff hung along the walls but, despite this impressive history, the place had retained its quaint charm. Just walking and talking to the musicians and sound folks would be fun, taking in the history, music and stories.

He peered into the glass recording studio, where a tall woman wearing white headphones was joking with one of the engineers. A guitarist, bass player, two horn players, a drummer, and a pianist were testing licks and arrangements in the dark cool room. "Right at this point of the build," the American woman began, looking up from the music she'd composed. "Come in *here* with the chord reprise,' she pointed, beginning to sing. 'How do you like it? How do you like it? *Deep, Deep, Deep.*'

She paused, looking to the piano player. "Does it sound right? I'm new at this but it's so cool." She laughed like a little girl, her voice magnified by the mics in the dark. Then she spun around at the sight of Christian, standing outside of the glass recording space, flustered by the presence of a stranger. "Hi, I'm Angie. We'll be done shortly. One more take. Sorry if you have it booked."

"No, no, no," Christian said. "Take your time, get it right. I'm just a tourist with time on his hands."

Angie looked up from the sheet of music in her hand and smiled. "Oh, thanks so much. I never realized how much goes into a recording," she giggled, "but these guys are showing me the ropes."

"You have beginner's luck then. The bit I heard was catchy," Christian said. The woman looked to be in her late twenties, attractive, but he couldn't place her name or face. The studio musicians were clearly enjoying the extra work, a nice change from pounding out a real-estate jingle, another kitschy remake of, 'You Can Get it If You Really Want It.' There was something about this woman's song, *Deep, deep, deep,* Christian smiled, listening to the back and forth. Was the song about what it sounded like?

"Thank you," she answered. "I want catchy, sexy too! I like the hook and the chorus, but it needs more. I want people to get up to dance, get people moving."

"Ma'am?" one of the engineers asked. "Is this song about what I think it is?"

"Yes," she chuckled. "That's why it needs to be energetic. But smooth and sophisticated, too." She smiled at the group in mock innocence. "Maybe even a little raunchy?"

Christian gazed over at this outspoken woman ordering these confused men around. There was a catchy beat to the chorus and refrain. "You must be a New Yorker?"

"Yes," the woman answered, extending her hand. "I'm Angela from the East Village." Her grip was strong, long fingers with no nail polish.

"Christian. Upper East Side," he answered with a smile. "That's a very catchy track you've just recorded."

"Thank you. I'm here doing a commercial for a real estate company and we had extra time to record a song I wrote a few months ago. It needs work, but at least I have a track to start from."

"So, what are you doing this afternoon?" Christian asked.

"Hopefully sitting in the warm sun. I'm headed back to New York in the morning, where it's 26 degrees and windy."

"Well, please come out to Half-Moon Bay. It's lovely and quiet and the views from the cottage we are in are stunning. Montego Bay is spectacular. Kingston's not exactly a paradise, except of course for music lovers. I have a great collection of reggae records, all recorded in this studio. Two of the guys on your record played with Desmond Decker and the Aces."

Angie beamed, she was leaving the studio with a heavy tin canister filled with reels of audiotape. She hoisted it on her hip, like a baby. They'd knocked out the commercial track in three takes, so the rest of the studio time was hers. Now she had to figure out what to do with it.

"I promise to get you to your flight in the morning. I'm here with a friend from New York, who's catching that morning flight to Kennedy. You'll like Carlos. He's done a bunch of commercials, too."

There was something so straightforward, positive, and trustworthy about this guy that made Angie instantly say 'yes.' She didn't feel the need to be cautious. Christian was gentle and asked questions, unlike most of the men she'd met.

"Wonderful," he answered. "My driver Ernest is outside, and he'll get you to your plane on time tomorrow early morning. I promise. … and I don't bite. Can I help you with that oversized tin can?"

"Yes, you may," Angie answered with a giggle. "Just don't drop it. It's my life savings."

"That record's gonna be a hit. Mark my words. I have a good sense for this."

Nineteen

The drive along the Montego Bay shoreline was like nothing Angie had ever experienced. She'd never felt so happy and relaxed. As they headed south out of Kingston, she took in the lively street life, the bright blue ocean, and the manicured beachfront enclaves. "So tell me," she chuckled. "Do you come here often?"

Christian smiled at the question. "As much as I possibly can, which amounts to a few weeks a year, *if* my parents invite me. They started coming here in the fifties when it opened. Before his inauguration, President Kennedy spent a night in that cottage," he said, pointing to a modest bungalow amid the palm trees, set back from the beach. "Supposedly Jackie wrote her will there."

"Did your parents know them?" she asked.

"Back then, everyone knew everyone. It's not as quaint as it used to be, but still laid-back. The food's better." When the driver reached Half Moon Bay, they parked in front of a cottage overlooking the water. Carlos waved from the deck. "He's been working on his tan. We don't do much around here. Sunbathing, reading, and the occasional island spliff. I was hoping he'd picked up some grouper to grill tonight."

Christian led her into the cottage and up a set of stairs, through the white slipcovered living room, and out onto the deck. She'd never seen so much blue ocean. "Carlos! I'd like you to meet Angie, I found her in town recording a smash hit record. She's the next big thing. I'm letting you in on it first."

Carlos stood and extended his hand. "It's a pleasure." Fit and handsome, he wore a Catalina white terry robe over red Laguna swim trunks, bare chest glistening with tanning oil.

"Angie worked at Y&R—but don't hold that against her," Christian said. "I just heard her new song and she's about to be the next great pop star."

"Well, it's not quite a song yet," she said, suddenly bashful. "But we've lugged the demos here in this metal can."

The afternoon slid quietly into twilight as the three of them traded stories about the ad biz. Christian knew Norman Berry from reputation and, of course, he'd heard all about Steve Caputo. "We tried recruiting him a few years back. When he asked for a ridiculous amount of money, we pegged him for a star monster. I'd always heard he was an asshole. There's one at every agency. When I saw the stories in the *Post*, it didn't surprise me."

"Yeah, I saw those, too," Angie snickered, pleased at her handiwork.

Angie mentioned playing faux-mom roles in children's cereal ads, and Carlos lit up. "I just did a Pepsi commercial. Honestly, I drink Coke, but the gig paid well, so I'll drink whatever they tell me." He'd danced and swigged room-temperature Pepsi-Cola for a few hours. Carlos grew up near Washington Heights. He'd also played the shirtless Latino hunk in fragrance and fashion ads for Brut and Van Heusen.

The talk turned to music, CBGBs, and the new band Blondie. "I've watched her on stage," Angie said. "She captures the audience instantly—the bleached hair, the attitude, the clothes. She's good for women's lib." Angie looked up, relaxed and warmed by the sun. "How can I make this reel of tape into a hit?" she said, staring at the canister on the table. "And how can I ever perform like Blondie?"

"I have a producer friend in New York," Christian said. "He could turn it into a hit. Gregg Silver at Buddha Records is your man. Remember 'Green Tambourine?' Or "O-o-h Child' from the Five Stairsteps? He's worked on everything from Captain Beefheart to the Lemon Pipers. That's him." He continued.

"It needs a faster dance beat, more trumpets; the song should pulse just before the refrain. Like where you sing, *'But if you want to know/ How I really feel/ Just get the cameras rolling/ Get the action going/ Deep, deep, deep/ How do you like it? How do you like it?'* It needs that pay-off that gets people moving. It's not a reggae song. It's more like a command in a porno movie." He looked at Angie as she nodded, expertly lighting a joint in the light afternoon breeze.

She'd left the studio with a master of 'Deep, Deep, Deep' for $750. The studio musicians didn't charge her extra for the three-hour recording session; now if she could finish it in New York and get it released, she might have a chance. 'I guess this is how pop music careers get started,' she thought. The Jamaican pot had sent Angie into the make-believe world of chart-topping music success. These lovely strangers were *so* encouraging. She gazed across the bright blue water feeling hopeful, even important, for once.

"Call me when you get back. I'll help set something up with Gregg. You'll like him." Christian had never claimed to be a music promoter, but there was something about Angie's breathy, seductive, ever-so-slightly off-key pacing in the cooing segments that made the song work. It was sexy, a bit naughty, with lyrics that unapologetically referenced Angie's past movie career.

"Where are you from?" Christian asked. "It's not a Cali voice, but it's western."

"Guess!"

"Seattle or Portland? It's indistinctly American, almost Canadian without the 'ehs.'"

"Close," she said. "Idaho. Mormon country."

"No! *Really?* You're the first person I've met from Idaho," Christian replied.

"We've got Sun Valley and potatoes. And some crazy Latter-Day Saints. That's about it," she answered quietly.

Christian smiled. "You okay?" he asked.

"Actually, I'm great," Angie answered, wiping her eyes. "I guess I'm a little stoned. This stuff is better than anything I've found in New York. I've got my future in that tin can and I guess my mind's going in twenty different directions."

Christian looked over at Angie. He'd had his fill of bull shitters. Heck, he peddled bullshit himself. Angie was transparent. Honest. Refreshing. She'd make a lousy poker player. "What made you leave?"

Twenty

Angie's words hung in the sweet, thick air for what seemed like hours. "I'm so sorry. I can't imagine what you've been through," Christian said.

He knew he'd have folded like a lawn chair if faced with the same challenges Angie had overcome. While Christian was swanning around at black tie balls, flirting with Marge's coterie of socialites, Angie was working menial jobs to survive. Her grit was as impressive as her talent, which he'd seen on full display today. "What did your parents say? Did you tell them?"

"I tried, but nobody even thought to ask if I was okay. The Mormon faith is all about conformity. Thank goodness I got out. I've often thought the *worst* thing that happened to me was also the *best*. My grandmother paid my way through Katie Gibbs, which got me to Y&R. She had my back when nobody else did. Even now, it's a little dicey out there. I was grateful for this gig. So, here I am, bruised but getting by."

"You're really brave," he said. She smiled, a little embarrassed at her candor, but she could feel these two nice men were safe, probably lovers. Still, they'd taken the time to ask and they genuinely seemed to care.

Christian looked over at this woman who had worked so hard. Unlike him, he could instantly tell that nothing had ever fallen into her lap. He'd never met anyone like her. She was so American – tall, outspoken, and independent with tenacity that fueled dreams he couldn't imagine. She lived life on the wild side. Her metal case and recording tape were sitting right beside her, her hand close by, her future in a can.

A week later, back in New York, Angie paid a visit to Gregg Silver in his studio on Seventh Avenue. 'Just out of curiosity," he asked her. "I wanted to take a couple of phrases out of the song and I realized that's the only verse."

"Which phrase?" she asked.

"You know, the one 'with the cameras rolling'? It doesn't make any sense."

"Well, do you know what I did?"

"Well obviously, you're the singer," he teased.

"Exactly," she beamed. "Everyone deserves to be celebrated in a song."

Sliver would later tell the *Times* reporter that, "she never suggested the lyrics were a reference to her film work, or *that* industry. It was just something she made up. She liked the hokey Herb Alpert-ish trumpet solo and that infectious raw beat of the demo."

By mid-February, Silver had produced a limited number of sample discs and sent her out to deliver them to deejays, clubs, and music publications. "This is where the business gets fun," he told her. "We gotta sell records and get people excited. Every good song needs a story."

Angie walked the vinyl samples all over Manhattan that winter. The disco clubs were the first to notice the track's infectious dance-floor draw. Radio airplay soon followed, spurring record sales. In a promotional video, Angie performed the song in a club wearing a white suede fringe jacket and hot pants. She bopped back and forth staring hypnotically into the camera as a disco ball above her sparkled, lit by multicolored strobe lights.

The single debuted on *Billboard*'s pop chart in the spring and, by June, it was a certified smash. 'Deep, Deep, Deep' played on steady rotation at nearly every pop station. Its six-minute extended version became a certified club classic. It was Angela's dream come true. "What makes me happy is seeing people dancing to it," she said in an interview with *Billboard*. "Looking out at an audience having the time of their lives is what I've always dreamed of."

Their lost afternoon at Half Moon Bay prompted Christian to call and ask her to dinner. He knew plenty of artists and writers and dreamers. But none of them matched this scrappy singer. He liked that she'd recorded it at Federal Records, courtesy of the Jamaican tourism board. He'd noticed her poise in television interviews.

Angie looked directly into the camera, smiled, and answered questions honestly, a few probably too honestly. Her background in making adult movies had surfaced, so her long plain pretty face was everywhere, and she talked openly about it to everyone who asked, including *The New York Times*.

"Is the song about your movie career?"

"Yes, and life in general, I guess. It's easy to skim the surface, but satisfaction comes from depth and hard work."

"What's it like having instant success?"

"My instant success came from a decade of hard work."

"Are you ashamed of acting in adult movies? You've been prolific."

"Not at all. Sex is sex. I lost my virginity to a rapist. Morality and 'saving it' for marriage is not part of my story. Most people like sex and I got paid well."

"Did you know you are the first adult star to have a number one song?

"No, but I hope many more talented women will step forward in the future. America is the land of opportunity, right?"

After the *New York Times* article, Angie's name would forever be preceded by the words 'porno-star turned pop-singer.' In truth, she regretted her porno movies, particularly now that her singing career had taken off. But she became an outspoken advocate for a profession long shunned. "The simple fact is the income from the movies paid for the voice lessons that resulted in a number one hit. Moving up the ladder, as it were," she was quoted in the article.

Angie took a more nuanced view of the article, now. "I think the *Times* reporter and the readers, assumed everyone had a pot of money lying around to jump-start a music career. Behind every one-hit wonder is a long and twisted road with lots of disappointments."

She'd received a flurry of calls to do more movies, with *her* soundtrack on it. "Are you interested? We'll pay you a hundred grand up front for a song and a fuck scene. You can be executive producer."

The money, at least, was tempting. But Angie didn't want to do another movie. She was sure she had another hit in her head and, nearing thirty, she deserved to cut ties with that world, particularly now. She could take a break, listen to music, maybe go to school? What came next would find her, not the other way around.

Dear Nana:

You're not going to believe it but I have a hit record on the Billboard charts. I have an agent, too. I started writing songs and singing in bands and turns out, I'm not bad at it. I'm not like a big star or anything, but it's neat having people say nice things to you.

I was in Jamaica shooting a commercial (doesn't that sound important? Ha ha) and I recorded this dance song I'd written. It was cheap to make and it's now a number #1 hit!!! I still can't believe it, it's like a dream I never dared to imagine. I met a nice guy who works for an ad agency (not the jerk) and he's helped me with music and promotion, which I don't have a clue about. I'll call. Lots to catch up on.

Love, Angie

Christian invited Angie to meet his parents at their apartment on 89th and Madison. He knew Marge would be a fan. He still couldn't get over walking into this old studio in Kingston and discovering this remarkable blond woman bossing musicians around to record a number one disco hit.

Marge had reserved a table at the Carlyle for Bobby Short's 10 o'clock show. Duella was coming, lured by the possibility that Christian was interested in a woman. He'd never picked a lane when it came to sex; he liked them both. So, the household was aflutter with curiosity about this woman who'd turned his head.

A night out with Bobby, Beverly, and Richard was the right time to meet this new lady. Isaac begged off. He'd just complain about the crowds and the cheap perfume permeating Bemelmans Bar these days. Bobby had filmed a commercial for Charlie, a new fragrance from Charles Revson. A big seller, the ad had attracted a lot of tourists to the old money saloon. Now, scoring a table to see Bobby required calling ahead and a $20 handshake upon arrival.

Marge and Angie bonded instantly. She needn't have worried. "It looks like fun," Marge said of her 'film' career. "Especially if you got one of those real hung Tarzan boys banging on you." Marge was a vocal advocate of 'free love' as she called it and predicted sex movies would soon go mainstream. "It's healthier than trysts and they're no wardrobe expenses. There are worse things than a naked man with a big boner going at it."

When the gin flowed, Marge was a colorful storyteller. She let on that she and Isaac 'weren't banging much' these days. Angie had been a nervous wreck in the week leading up to their meeting, worried she'd say something stupid. Christian assured her his parents were 'down to earth', but she knew they were fancy, nevertheless. Christian had described his father as 'noble but flinty' and his mother as 'a piece of work' that defied explanation. *You'll be fine, I promise.*

Duella Graves was joining them tonight. Christian was insistent that she and Angie meet. "Bobby may be high society now, but I met him in the forties when he came to New York," Duella said. "Lovely man and nobody can play Eubie, Fats, Duke or Billy Strayhorn like him. It's music that no one plays anymore. I'm proud of him. He's done well for our people."

Marge had seen Short play back when he was a child star in Chicago. At fourteen, he was as poised and stylish as any performer she'd ever met. He stuck with it, paid his dues, and now sat at the throne adored by New York high society. "I've got beginner's luck," he began on the piano to cheery claps, "the moment I fell in love, I fell in love with you. Aren't I fortunate?"

Success with 'Deep, Deep, Deep' spread to the UK charts, where it climbed to #5, and throughout Europe and South America, it scored in the top ten. Angie recorded vocals for a Spanish language mix called 'Profunda, Profunda, Profunda.' The Latin market single jacket featured a picture of Angie wearing her signature fringe outfit while feeding a small farm animal. With 'Deep, Deep, Deep' climbing the charts, Buddha Records went quickly to work on getting an album into production in New York.

Gregg Silver composed and produced all the tracks, which were largely long instrumental concoctions. Angela was dressed in a more conservative non-revealing pair of outfits for the record jacket covers. But the end-product was rushed. The album cuts, though melodic and well-rendered, didn't have the immediate hook as 'Deep, Deep, Deep.' Some manufacturing runs featured inaccurate track listings.

"It was a mess," Silver admitted later. "It didn't sound like it was mixed. I tried to make sense of it but, mind you, I only had a weekend to do it. Buddha needed it by Monday morning, or they would miss this whole production run thing. You don't want to lose momentum when the record is number one. You want to put an LP out there."

In late summer, one track called 'Party Train' was released as a single and marketed to clubs and radio stations. Angie performed the song and other cuts on prominent music shows like *Rock Concert* and she smiled enthusiastically, giving it her all. Still, she nervously tugged at microphone cords, while carefully watching her footing on the reflective revolving floor as confetti fell from above the stage. The song fared well in clubs, but the album was a disappointment, peaking at 83 on the *Billboard* pop albums chart. Within months, copies turned up for $2.99 in cut-rate bins at record stores.

It had gotten to be late afternoon and Angie had poured a glass of wine. The spring day had spun away in the best of ways, for the best of reasons. "I continued working on new music, to prove my fluke hit wasn't a fluke. But my voice wasn't exactly Whitney Houston's," she smiled. "It had been over a year since the song hit and I knew I had to have a follow-up. Disco music wore thin unless you were on the dance floor. I wanted to explore other genres and styles, despite everyone around me pleading for another hit."

"I also got six-figure offers to make one more high-end porno movie where I'd write and perform the soundtrack. It was tempting but I just couldn't do it. It was a very heady time and I remember it like it was yesterday."

"The hard part, as Clara knows well, was becoming semi-famous for a very short time when my past movie career resurfaced. I wasn't ashamed, although I worried how my family would handle it, take the attention. They were Latter Day Saints after all! Would they be ostracized because of my movies? That I genuinely worried over and had no clue of what would happen. I mentioned unintended consequences before. My temporary musical fame was discounted because of the porno movies. It was always 'pop singer and porno star Angela Love' in articles. My bad, I guess.

"It doesn't matter now, but reputation remains the snapshot summary of us as people." She shrugged, accepting the situation, having thought about this more than once.

At that point, Clara jumped in. "I was really young, maybe thirteen or fourteen, but my parents and cousins treated my aunt's success with disgrace. It was a knee jerk reaction. It was never how proud they were that a hometown girl had gone to the big city and done well; creating a number one hit, for Christ sakes! It was always that apologetic whisper of the porno career and the disappointed head shaking that was their lead headline."

She took a deep breath, pausing. "I personally found your success motivating and it made me want to do something different and get the hell away from Idaho. I'd learned not to be judgmental," Clara she slowly giggled. "And game for new things and experiences."

"Andy's people contacted me about a movie," Angie began. "I was flattered that he would consider making a movie about my life. He talked it up, assuring me this would be a masterpiece, his last movie. He told me he was done with experimentation. Blah, blah, fucking, blah. Andy was blowing smoke in his soft-spoken weird passive-aggressive way. He was a salesman, and he was looking for redemption. 'Ciao Manhattan' was a mess." Angie took a deep breath, realizing that no one knew what she was talking about.

'Ciao Manhattan' had been conceived as a snapshot of the 60's underground seen through Edie's cockeyed lens. It turned out to be a disaster. Even by Andy's loose standards, the movie was incoherent and the production reckless. Edie had been off the rails for several months and couldn't function without a steady stream of amphetamines. "I hadn't kept up with her over the past few years, but she was completely out-of-control. Like everyone else who worked for Andy in that era, he got richer and everyone else fell apart.

"For one scene," Angie continued shaking her head, "the coked-out cinematographer straddled himself on the hood of a car to shoot Edie speeding over the George Washington Bridge, after she'd been awake for three days, propelled by speed-laced vitamin shots. In another scene, one of the stars is supposed to drive around the Pan Am Building near Grand Central Terminal. Instead, as he neared the camera, he threw the script out the window, and kept driving. No one heard from him for eighteen months, at which point he's in a Michigan jail.

"You couldn't make this stuff up. It was crazy time that people saw as artistic genius and acceptable behavior. I blame Andy for letting it get out of hand, but he wasn't right either. Getting shot completely changed him, physically and mentally. Everyone was becoming a casualty." Angie paused, remembering the stories she'd heard about the movie. Then she continued slowly. "The final day of shooting turned into an orgy after the entire cast dropped acid. Before the movie was released, Edie disappeared to California never to be seen again."

Andy wanted to return to making movies, his first love. His new idea was to make an old-fashioned New York romantic love story based on Angie. This movie would be everything that 'Ciao Manhattan' wasn't. It was a familiar tale like his, a creative striver from the provinces who comes to New York to seek fame and fortune. Now she was a disco queen with a top hit. What a perfect character for this era! The movie would be called 'Hello New York.'

Now at aged forty-eight, Andy constantly dreamed about death. He also was making ridiculous money painting colorful portraits of celebrities that he could resell for more as signed lithographs. Andy had always talked about 'art for the masses', but he couldn't have imagined his work would go for the prices he could charge nowadays.

"Now is the time to make my movie," I remember him telling me. "My brand is hot! I'll do it right this time and bring in a named director and produce a real movie," he told Fred Hughes, his business manager. "Hello New York' will be my cinematic masterpiece, my statement about the American Dream. I just need to find the right girl to play you. Peggy Lipton is worth a try – right cool, right looks? Maybe Susan Dey? She's sexy and sang in 'The Partridge Family.' Maybe Sidney Lumet would do it? Or Mike

Nichols?" Andy could finally make his signature movie about fame and personal brand, even though the line between art and life had completely blurred for him by this point."

"So, what was Andy Warhol like as a person?" May asked eagerly. Real or imagined interactions with Andy and his pack of misfit toys had been a part of Angie's life for over a decade, although she had drifted away from The Factory over the past few years as her music career began to blossom.

Angie smiled, thinking for a bit. "He recognized that he had more value as an image than as a real person with a private life," she began. "He was a capitalist who understood popular culture." Angie spoke slowly and carefully, not trying to sensationally pile on to his reputation which had continued to grow since his death over a decade ago. "He was a strange distant man who somehow captured what people wanted in art and in an artistic celebrity."

She paused, trying to stay with her train of thought, realizing she was talking to a *Rolling Stone* reporter. The last thing she wanted was to trash the era's most famous artist. "There were times Andy was original and brilliant, seeing things no one else had, and making them important. He liked to call himself a 'business artist who didn't starve.'

"We talked for a few years about doing a movie after 'Deep, Deep, Deep' came out, but I had no interest in reliving my adult movie career in the hands of Andy Warhol. He really wasn't interested either. It was one of my few prudent decisions in that period," she chuckled. "Falling in love with Christian, the other.'"

Angie stood up and wandered over to the bookshelves behind the piano. It was strewn with Christian's pictures, magazines, books, and mementoes she had pulled out to remind herself about his love of wandering the world for all those years. "Christian was a pack rat and I've never had the energy to try to sort through and catalog all of it, except what you see. I've saved very little, except this nice little drawing Andy gave me after I did that first silly movie in the bathtub that got me in hot water."

She returned with a small pen and ink sketch that Andy had drawn while filming 'Spa Boy.' "I never showed this to anyone besides Christian, but I love it. It captures the moment in time perfectly, 1970, she laughed. "Why I was getting filmed lying naked in a bathtub is a subject for another day. I'm exhausted, let's go to bed."

Twenty-One

"We talked about Christian a little," May began the next morning. She saw a love story within the one-hit wonder story. Angie and Christian were more human and interesting than any music story she'd covered. This wasn't about trashing hotel rooms or snorting cocaine off of framed pictures and glass tables.

"One of the first things I remember about Christian before we were married was his lifelong work for the City of New York. This family were old-fashioned civitans. He mobilized music concerts and put records on the back of cereal boxes; but his greatest accomplishment was turning around perceptions of New York City."

She poured a large cup of coffee and smeared cream cheese on her poppy seed bagel. "In the late seventies, the city had hit rock bottom."

"I read about our bicentennial, how it almost broke the back of New York City," May interjected. "What do you remember about the summer of '76?"

"All of it!" Angie answered, getting up to retrieve the big box in the closet. "I saved letters and copies of the New York *Daily News*," she continued. "Look at this one!" she said. The cover page showed the handwritten note sent to columnist Jimmy Breslin by the serial murderer, Son of Sam. Breslin had begun communicating with him, through his column. The note read:

Hello from the gutters of N.Y.C. which are filled with dog manure, vomit, stale wine, urine, and blood. Hello from the sewers of N.Y.C. which swallow up these delicacies when they are washed away by the sweeper trucks. Hello from the cracks in the sidewalks of N.Y.C. and from the ants that dwell in these cracks and feed in the dried blood of the dead that has settled into the cracks.

PS: Please inform all the detectives working the slaying to remain. P.S: JB, please inform all the detectives working the case that I wish them the best of luck. Keep 'em digging, drive on, think positive, get off your butts, knock on coffins, etc." Upon my capture I promise to buy all the guys working the case a new pair of shoes if I can get up the money. Son of Sam

"Everyone was scared. Nothing worked," Angie continued, flipping through the old tabloid. "Look at this!" she pointed at a headline: 'Headless Body Found in Topless Bar.' "Nothing surprised anyone during this time. The rules were out the door. New York was wild and dangerous back then."

For the past twelve months a serial killer, New York's first since the 1930s, had been preying on young women (brunettes, specifically), mostly in Queens. The pattern was hard to ignore. The victims, all young women or couples, all from the outer boroughs, had all been shot with a .44 caliber Charter Arms revolver.

Conclusive proof came when the killer struck in Forest Hills Gardens in early March. The victim, a Columbia student, was walking from the subway after sunset. As she turned onto her street, headed home, a man jumped in front of her and fired. The bullet extracted from her head matched the slugs from the prior five unsolved murders, confirming that all had been issued from the same .44 caliber revolver.

Six weeks later, the .44-caliber killer returned to the North Bronx. The victims were parked in a Mercury Montego on a dark service road off the Hutchinson River Parkway. When the detectives pulled the bodies out of the car, an envelope addressed to the NYPD fell to the ground. Inside was a four-page handwritten letter written in neat, slanted block letters: *I'LL BE BACK.*

Leads were scarce. The police task force tried everything from bringing in psycholinguists to study the handwriting to psychiatrists analyzing the content. The ensuing profile – 'the killer is a paranoid schizophrenic, a loner who lives in a cheap furnished room who feels rejected by women and may even consider himself possessed' – didn't help investigators much. But when this profile was leaked in the press, the suspect became enraged.

The NYPD brought in a psychic to the various crime scenes, read tracts on demonic possession, even studied the Bible looking for clues. They enlisted astrologists to decode the strange symbols adorning the letter, with the movement of the stars. The killer claimed to be directed by a father figure named Sam. He was Sam's son. What did that mean? Was he a Vietnam veteran, a son of Uncle Sam? Was Sam a reference to Satan? Samson? Or to Sam Colt, the inventor of the gun he used? Several survivors saw their attacker fire his weapon with both hands, the stance taught at the Police Academy. Could the killer be a laid-off cop?

Fifty city detectives were working the case, with twenty more on standby, and well over a hundred uniformed and undercover officers were involved. Another seven hundred cops volunteered for duty in their off-hours, making this the largest manhunt in New York history. By the middle of July, the task force was receiving a thousand tips a day.

On July 28, the day before the anniversary of the first attack, the *Daily News* printed Breslin's 'Son of Sam' column on its front page. Breslin dedicated the column to the killer, marking his 'his first death day' and resurrecting the letter he'd sent two months earlier, hoping to force a crack in the case. The following night, the killer struck for the eighth time, killing a twenty-year-old couple. Like the tidal wave of looting and arson that would accompany the blackout, the .44 caliber killer hysteria had created a deep fear among New Yorkers.

On August 1st, a young cop issued a parking ticket in Yonkers. One of them, for thirty-five dollars, traced a cream-colored Ford Galaxy sedan to David Berkowitz of 35 Pine Street in Yonkers. The car stood too close to a fire hydrant, posing a danger. But calls to Berkowitz's residence went unanswered.

Detectives made their way toward Yonkers, a bleak city of boarded-up red brick factories, bordering Westchester County. They found the car at his address and noticed an army duffle in the backseat containing a rifle, a toothbrush, and a pair of dirty Jockey shorts. In the glove box was a letter addressed to the Suffolk County Police Department, promising an attack at a disco in the Hamptons.

As the officers assembled outside, Berkowitz remained upstairs in his $238-a-month studio. The place was furnished with a box spring on a shag rug. Manic red scribblings covered the walls and pornographic magazines were strewn across the floor. Dirty sheets hung over the windows, obscuring the view of the Hudson River.

That night, Berkowitz emerged from the building at 10:30 p.m. wearing frayed jeans, tennis shoes, and a wrinkled light blue sports shirt. The detectives moved quickly, guns drawn, as Berkowitz got in the car and started the engine. "Turn off the ignition and step out of the car."

"You got me," Berkowitz told the cop.

"Who are you?"

"You know me."

"I don't."

"I'm the Son of Sam."

Twenty-Two

The city went dark just after 9:30 p.m. on July 13, 1977. At first, people wondered if they'd forgotten to pay their utility bill. "Didn't they get my check?" one Bronx housewife asked. Others were afraid. A teenager at the movies in Queens panicked that the serial killer turned out the lights before striking again. A sixty-four-year-old woman thought she'd suddenly gone blind. She, and everyone else, would discover the city's grid had shut down, overloaded after a severe thunderstorm had disabled two generators in Westchester County.

The darkness was surreal and oddly beautiful. *Daily News* columnist Pete Hamill wrote, "The Brooklyn Bridge was dark, the skyline was gone, and the only light came from a dull glow over New Jersey. Over to the left, you could see the Statue of Liberty, still lit up in the harbor like a small green toy." The Mets-Cubs game at Shea Stadium was halted in the sixth inning and the ballet at Lincoln Center stopped. The cast members of 'Oh Calcutta,' unable to get to the dressing room, were stranded onstage, nude, until audience members lent them clothes.

The sudden darkness created opportunity. The baubles in store windows were suddenly within reach. Anyone could stretch out a hand and grab sneakers, stereos, jewelry, and color televisions with little sanction. What difference did it make? The white store owners would collect insurance and move on.

Police officers watched as hundreds of shoppers milling about an A&P store in Broo.klyn, scrambled to take what food remained on the shelves. "How can you shoot anyone here?" one officer asked. "For every twenty we lock up, fifty more will take their place." One looter said, "It was like the man upstairs said, 'I'm gonna put the lights out for twenty-four hours and you all go off ... get everything you can."

The loss of power was less significant than the massive theft and property damage. Looting was the natural, if illegal, response to the rising unemployment and deepening poverty among working-class New Yorkers. The city had become partitioned and ungovernable. People were scared. The darkness illuminated the desperate state of New York's ghettos, where black and Hispanic teenage unemployment was hovering at 75%. The blackout took the city's failings public, exposing the truth to the rest of the country.

Racial and class tensions, long simmering, boiled over. Guests at a ritzy birthday party at the St. Moritz Hotel thought it was just part of the festivities, the lights turned off for the cutting of the cake. Upper East Side restaurants that lost air conditioning quickly set up tables outside for alfresco dining. The looting and crime was happening in poor black neighborhoods. In Brooklyn and the Bronx, among the 1600 stores robbed, a Pontiac dealership was relieved of fifty new cars, after the showroom's plate glass windows were shattered.

New Yorkers knew their city was a broken, dysfunctional welfare state. The blackout was just another visible symptom. Of those arrested, 65 percent were black, 30 percent Latino, and 4 percent white. Only 8 percent were age 40 or over; and only 7 percent were women.

"All those who thought we should have called in the National Guard during the blackout, raise your hand!" Ed Koch bellowed through a battery-powered bullhorn, thrusting his right hand into the air. "All those who are in favor of capital punishment, raise your hand." The candidate's bald head glistened with sweat as he stood before a growing crowd of weary Staten Island commuters at the Battery Park ferry terminal, weary from a long August workday. "Society has the right to express its moral outrage."

Koch was certainly expressing his. While Abe Beame campaigned against Con Edison in the weeks following the blackout, Koch called for the Police Commissioner's resignation and asked why the mayor failed to summon the National Guard to help maintain order. Reviving capital punishment had become a hot idea, particularly in the outer boroughs where the Son of Sam prowled for victims. In all, 62 percent the city favored reinstituting the death penalty with only 24 percent opposed. Koch took his appeal across the city to senior centers in Staten Island, beach clubs and boardwalks of Brooklyn and Queens, and nursing homes in the Bronx.

Abe Beame, the incumbent, dismissed his mayoral opponent as a Greenwich Village liberal and political opportunist, pandering to the feral mood in the city. Koch promised to protect middle-class neighborhoods from 'the nuts on the left' and criticized the 'poverticians.' He championed capital punishment, pummeled the unions, and railed against government waste—not a typical liberal platform. Even William F. Buckley called Koch 'a liberal in the actuarial sense of the word, but a man who had already been ready to look ideology in the face long enough to recognize its glass eye.'

More than two months after New York's long night of looting and damage, *New York Post* writer Pete Hamill commented, "This is the city that Ed Koch will have to cure – a city abandoned, a city unrepresented, a cynical city, the ruined and broken city." No longer was New York going to be run by labor bosses, political power brokers and social visionaries. It wasn't a ruined and broken mess any longer, but the place to go to 'make it.' The future belonged to entrepreneurs and to the private sector. New players like George Steinbrenner, Reggie Jackson, Donald Trump, and Rupert Murdoch emerged to lead the city forward.

Twenty-Three

He was part old-fashioned ballplayer – 'an uninhibited colossus of a man' wrote Harry Stein in *Esquire* – 'and part newfangled black superstar in designer jeans, snug-fitting turtlenecks and Italian loafers with a male purse tucked under his muscular arm.' He was the national pastime's first made-for-TV celebrity. But he wasn't famous enough for his own taste. "I want to be nationally known," he proclaimed after his team, the Oakland Athletics won its third straight World Series in 1974. "I'm not a household name yet."

Reggie Jackson had come a long way since he batted .300 for the Class A Lewiston Broncs of the Northwest League, where he hit a memorable dinger that broke a window in a little house across the street from the ballpark. Angie remembered that Saturday afternoon in 1965 like it was yesterday. Much of the reason she was in New York was because of small-minded gossips in town spreading ridiculous rumors about her and Reggie Jackson. New York truly was the land of lost and found toys. At least they were headed in the same direction.

He had come to New York for a job interview and was meeting his future boss, George Steinbrenner at the 21 Club. Jackson wasn't impressed with the checkered table cloths and cheap-looking furniture. It looked like a saloon, rather than a fancy restaurant. The floor wasn't even carpeted. The word was that baseball's number one free agent was looking for $3 million for five years, an unprecedented amount.

"It's not just about the money," Steinbrenner began his pitch. "It's about your life here. You are in the prime of your career and deserve the best city and best fans. You can have an apartment in a tony Upper East Side building with a sweeping view of Central Park. It's an easy drive to the ballpark and this city is full of fine restaurants and beautiful sophisticated women. The way you talk," he added. "Dealing with the media will be like eating ice cream."

They took a slow walk up Fifth Avenue, passing by hansom cabs in front of the Plaza Hotel before turning north on Madison Avenue. It was a beautiful, warm November day to sell a famous potential resident on big, bustling, cultured and glamorous New York City. "I had been there before, but really hadn't been there before," Jackson remembered. "It was as if I had seen New York across a crowded room, caught her eye, but never got a chance to talk to her. Now I was talking to her, feeling her. Being seduced by her."

Even the editorial page of the *New York Times* took note of his arrival in town. "Reggie Jackson is a flamboyant man whose self-confidence is matched only by his athletic ability. By choosing New York, Jackson has become the

Yankees first black superstar, not to mention their first black millionaire."

The New York Yankees manager, Billy Martin, followed the Steinbrenner-Jackson courtship in the papers with a growing sense of disgust. Reggie was the kind of player who liked to draw attention to himself; the kind of player that Martin tended not to like, and over the years he'd directed more than one of his pitchers to throw at Jackson. What bothered Martin was all the attention that Steinbrenner had lavished on him. "George was taking Reggie to the 21 Club for lunch all of the time and I was sitting in my hotel room the entire winter and George hadn't taken me out to lunch even once."

If Billy Martin was looking for a reason to mistrust the newest member of his team, he didn't need to look far. Jackson told one of the reporters that he was excited about coming to New York because 'he and George got along so well.' *You're going to find out that George isn't the manager*, Martin thought to himself.

Jackson also got off on the wrong foot with captain Thurman Munson. "Hey, you have to run now," he told Reggie, as the slugger made his way to the batting cage. "The way we do it here, you run before you hit."

"Yeah," Jackson replied, attempting humor. "But if I run now, I'll be too tired to hit later."

"Yeah, but if you don't run now, it'll make a bad impression on the other players."

Thurman Munson was coming off one of the best seasons of his career. The Yankees' new captain – the team's first since Lou Gehrig – had just hit .302 with 105 RBIs and caught an astonishing 155 games, a performance that earned him the American League's Most Valuable Player award. After news of Jackson's signing broke, Munson reminded Steinbrenner that his contract stipulated he would be the team's highest-paid everyday player.

The matter seemed settled as Munson's salary was increased to $200,000, before he learned that Reggie's salary did not include deferred income ($132,000), a cash signing bonus ($400,00), an interest free loan ($1 million) or a custom Rolls-Royce Corniche ($93,000). An irritated Steinbrenner replied, "My promise was that no Yankee regular would be paid more annually in his *weekly checks* than Thurman was." The discussion was over.

The best-paid man in baseball started the 1977 season slowly. Six weeks into the season, Jackson was hitting .250 with only five home runs. And he struggled defensively in the outfield. He had discussed putting his name on a candy bar, only to be ridiculed in the press about one named 'Butterfingers' already in the market. After one Sunday morning clubhouse chapel service on the road, he stuck around for a private session with the minister.

Emerging a half hour later, Reggie told writers that he felt much better. "I was reminded that when we lose and I strike out, a billion people in China don't care. But millions of New Yorkers do and they were letting me know it every time I waved at a bad pitch, grounded out, or bobbled a pop fly."

NBC's *Game of the Week* on June 17th was played between the Yankees and Boston Red Sox on a still, sweltering day at Fenway Park. Twenty-five million people had tuned in to the broadcast between the league-leading Red Sox and their hated rivals. At the bottom of the sixth inning with the Red Sox leading 7-4, announcer Phil Rizzuto commented, "Uh oh, it looks like Billy's calling Paul Blair to replace Jackson and Jackson doesn't know it yet. We're liable to see a little display of temper here … it's Reggie's fault for not hustling on the last play."

Rizzuto quickly searched his mind. He never recalled a manager making a defensive substitution in the middle of an inning.

"Oh, look at Billy!" Rizzuto barked. "Is he hot!" The Fenway crowd watched Blair trotting across the field toward Jackson.

Jackson looked up, pointing to himself in disbelief. "You mean me?" Blair nodded as they came together in right field. "What the hell is going on?"

Blair shrugged. "You've got to ask Billy that."

The NBC cameras followed Reggie trotting off the field and into the dugout. He looked more puzzled than angry, with his hands spread, palm side up, in an expression of confusion.

Martin was waiting for him, neck cords bulging and knees bent. "What the fuck do you think you're doing out there?" he asked.

"What do you mean? What are you talking about?"

"You know what the fuck I'm talking about. You want to show me up by loafing on me. Fine. Then I'm going to show your ass up. Anyone who doesn't hustle doesn't play for me."

Reggie stood stunned on the steps of the dugout. He took off his glasses and started moving towards Martin.

"They're gonna confront each other right there in the dugout!" *Game of the Week* announcer Joe Garagiola said excitedly, as NBC's cameras zoomed in. They were close enough for America to read Martin's lips: "I ought to kick your fucking ass."

"Who the fuck do you think you're talking to, old man?" Reggie spit back. "Don't you ever dare to show me up again, motherfucker."

Martin started toward Jackson. "There they go!" said Garagiola. Quickly one of the coaches grabbed Martin and pinned him against a pole. "Billy wants a little piece of Reggie Jackson." Two other coaches pulled Martin back into the dugout, out of camera range as things finally began to quiet down.

The Red Sox went on to win the game 10-4. Still hot, Martin fielded questions in Fenway's cramped visiting manager's office. "When a player shows up the team, I show up the player."

"Did you think twice about pulling Reggie in such a close game?"

"We won last year without him, didn't we?"

"Did you consider a more conventional means of discipline?"

"How do you fine a superstar? Take away his Rolls-Royce?"

"Do you think the incident was bad for baseball since the game was on national television?"

"I don't care if it went all over the world," Martin answered.

The image of a brawny black slugger, his glasses removed, standing chest to chest with his scrawny white manager was plastered on sports pages across the country. Very few people defended Reggie. Most New Yorkers were proud of Martin – their working class hero – for standing up to the arrogant, overpaid slugger.

Even his black teammate Chris Chambliss criticized him. "Reggie, you know what you'd be if you were white? Just another damn white boy. Be glad you are black getting all of this publicity you do, getting away with all the shit you do."

The city's black newspaper, the *Amsterdam News* piled on. "He says he wants to rebuild rundown Harlem since he hit town in April. But he's never taken the time to learn some of the problems of the community as he drives up

Madison Avenue from his $1500 per month apartment at 80th and Fifth Avenue in his $27,500 foreign-made car, across the 138th Street Bridge and into Yankee Stadium where he earns $400,000 per year as a diamond superstar. He lacks the inner qualities and charisma of Muhammed Ali, Joe Louis or Ray Robinson who were 'people's heroes."

Even before he was restrained from attacking his right fielder on national television, Billy Martin was having problems. His talented, heavily favored team was struggling to stay in the pennant race. Nearly all of his starting pitchers were getting lit up, and just about every southpaw in the league was shutting down his lefty-heavy lineup.

Reached in Cleveland for a comment after the incident, Steinbrenner sided with his high-paid slugger, telling the *Boston Globe* reporter that it didn't look to him that Reggie wasn't hustling. "What it looked like," he added, "is my ball club is out of control." The news wires began reporting that Martin was going to be fired and replaced by Yogi Berra.

Angry fans flooded Yankee Stadium and local radio and TV stations with calls. *Fire Martin and it will look as if Reggie runs the team.* Reggie too didn't want Martin fired, at least not on his account. He had enough problems without being blamed for costing the popular manager his job.

With all of the daily dramas, it was easy to overlook Reggie's statistical line moving past respectable and toward impressive. By August 5th, he was hitting .291 with eighteen home runs, ten stolen bases and fifty-eight RBIs, eleven of which were game winners. A week later, he found himself penciled into the clean-up slot and responded with a run-scoring single. On August 18th, his second day batting cleanup, Reggie singled home the winning run in a game in Oakland.

The next night, he exploded for four extra base hits and five RBIs in a doubleheader sweep on the California Angels. The following afternoon, Reggie showed off his once-feared arm, cutting down Bobby Bonds, one of the fastest men in baseball, on a throw from right field to the plate. The Yankees were finally winning without drama and suddenly they were in first place, having won fourteen of their last sixteen games to reach the World Series.

Martin's fleeting moment of contentment at having again skippered his team to the Series evaporated into a more familiar sentiment: underappreciation. He was happy to tell the press about the season's 'turning point' – standing up to Reggie in the dugout at Fenway.

And that if the Yankees went on to win the World Series, "Steinbrenner needs to sweeten my contract, or I'm planning to talk to other clubs. If he buys $50 million worth of players, I'll beat him with another club and he knows it. I'll make him cry."

Steinbrenner answered. "He's crazy if he tries to take credit for our success. I believe the team's turning point began on August 10 when I directed Billy to start hitting Reggie at cleanup. He's just trying to work up public support."

Public support was one thing that Billy Martin possessed. When he was introduced before Game One against the Los Angeles Dodgers in New York, the fans stood and cheered themselves hoarse. "This is in recognition of Billy telling off his boss," Dick Young of the *Daily News* wrote, "by 55,000 people who dream of telling off the boss." The teams had last met in the 1963 World Series, a Dodgers sweep.

It was a brisk night in New York and the Empire State Building was illuminated in blue and white. About an hour before the first pitch, a fire started in Public School 3, an abandoned elementary school a few blocks west of the stadium. By the time ABC's coverage began at 8 pm, orange flames were blazing upward toward the sky. The network cut to its camera in a helicopter hovering above for an aerial view. "There it is, ladies and gentlemen," announced Howard Cosell in his best melodramatic New York accent, "the Bronx is burning."

By the late innings, the fire had grown to five alarms. Play was halted repeatedly while stadium police chased fans from the field. Rolls of toilet paper, whiskey bottles and firecrackers rained down on the field. Upper deck patrons dumped beer on the box seat fans below. A policeman was assaulted when he asked several fans to lower a banner that was obstructing the view of those sitting behind them.

One fan pulled down his pants, another tossed a smoke bomb onto the field that beclouded the outfield in an eerie green haze. New York's national degradation wasn't complete until the final out of the game, when a fan pegged Dodgers' right fielder Reggie Smith in the head with a hard rubber ball. He required immediate medical attention and left town the next day in a neck brace.

A week later the Yankees held a three games to two lead, with the sixth game set for Yankee Stadium. The skies had cleared, but cool air lingered in the mid-fifties as the home team went out for batting practice at 6:30. Reggie Jackson stepped up to take his cuts and he smashed the first three pitches into the third tier of the right field bleachers, some 500 feet from home plate.

No one recalled how many Reggie hit out during batting practice, but everyone remembered it. "Every ball flew like it was shot out of a cannon," a teammate said. "It was an electrifying thing. People were completely amazed."

In the hours that followed, Reggie Jackson's performance overshadowed the ongoing melodrama that engulfed the 1977 New York Yankees season. He was simply super human. At the beginning of the fourth inning with the Yankees down 3-2, Jackson came to bat and tapped his bat lightly on the plate before hitting a low liner, not more than fifteen feet off the ground before it landed in the first row of the right field bleachers.

He circled the bases elegantly, his upper body bent forward, slowing to a trot as he approached home plate. Two innings later, he did exactly the same thing on the first pitch sending the screaming line drive into the stands. Between first and second base, he picked at his form fitting uniform as the crowd chanted 'Reggie, Reggie, Reggie.'

In the bottom of the eighth inning, a standing ovation greeted Jackson as he walked toward the plate. The din continued as he smoothed the dirt in the batter's box with his spikes. Then he reached down for the pitcher's diving knuckleball as the crowd fell silent, heard the crack, then watched the ball sail toward dead center, touching down about halfway up the stadium's blacked-out bleachers, some 475 feet from home plate, putting the Yankees on top 8-3. Only Babe Ruth had hit three home runs in a single World Series game, but never in consecutive at bats, let alone on just three pitches.

The tabloids wove Reggie's three home runs into a narrative of the city's struggle for survival. "Who dares to call New York a lost cause?" the *New York Post* editorialized. After antagonizing Jackson earlier in the season, the *Amsterdam News* now lauded him, comparing his game six feat to Jackie Robinson's first major league home run.

To Reggie Jackson, those home runs delivered a simple message: "Let me up now, I'm no longer going to be held down."

Twenty-Four

Christian had long known that New York needed an advertising campaign to draw tourists back to the city. He'd just joined Wells Rich Greene, but still had friends in the New York State Department of Commerce from the Harlem Nights evening. Beyond the blackout and Son of Sam murders, New York's brand had sunk into a dangerous shadow of its proud Empire State heritage. Even the NYPD had been handing out booklets titled 'Welcome to Fear City' at the airports to arriving passengers, in response to threats to cut their benefits.

"We need a plan," William Doyle, the State's marketing director and charming raconteur, told Christian, Governor Carey, and Mayor Koch. "We must squeeze money for tourism out of this penniless legislature with a good, foolproof plan. Just got word that Union Carbide is moving its headquarters out to Danbury. They explained the move saying no one wants to visit, let alone work here. I've never been one to piss away money—money we don't have—on intangibles, like branding and PR, whatever in the hell that is. But we have a big image problem that we must fix."

New York's marketing budget was the lowest per capita among all fifty states. The state, not just the city, had done a horrendous job of promoting its charms. The state's Department of Commerce finally agreed to allocate $4.3 million for an advertising campaign – but they'd need it done quickly. Spring advertising brought summer visitors. The first ads showed people from other states coming into New York: "I'm from Cape Cod, but I Love New York," or "If you love the outdoors, you'll love New York."

But New York needed more than a slogan and chirpy family visitors. The State of Virginia had launched their 'Virginia is for Lovers' campaign a decade ago. Love was in the air, if you could sort out where to go to find it. Governor Hugh Carey dismissed their concerns. "You know, Virginia claims it is the state for lovers, but when you drive through Virginia all they give you is a speeding ticket. New York is the state for lovers; I love it and I want everybody to love it. If I get you the money, will you come up with a campaign that makes *everybody* love New York?"

Doyle hired jingle writer Steve Karmen to set the campaign to music. Karmen got the music just right, simple, spiritual, memorable—and repetitive. The jingle lifted hearts and souls. To accompany the jingle, he suggested a stripped down message—'I Love New York'—and a logo to amplify it. "You need Milton Glaser," Karmen told Wells Rich Greene. "Best graphic designer in the world, and a New Yorker to boot. He did Bob Dylan's greatest hits album and developed *New York* magazine's design format. He'll get the right balance. We need a homerun." Christian was relieved to find allies in the trade, who saw the New York brand as the city's present lodestone ... and the flying kite to a successful future.

Two days later, Glaser, a slight, older man with an imposing bald pate, goatee and wry professional air arrived alone at the agency. He'd responded to Christian's and Mary Wells' last-minute call about helping to 'save our city.' The city team would arrive in the morning. *Could he be there at 9:00 sharp?*

For twenty years, Milton Glaser's Pushpin Studio in the East 20s had been the hot design destination. Glaser fully understood the challenge. He was no stranger to clients calling for last-minute logo ideas, but this request came with palpable urgency. Although a born and raised native, Milton Glaser knew New York was a hard sell. And politicians made for insecure clients. Like everyone else, he'd watched his hometown decline, with the last few years particularly dismal.

The collective eyes in the room all turned to the little man, as he pulled a folded sheet of hotel stationary out of his shirt pocket. On it was a doodle he'd done on the cab ride to the meeting. In red crayon, he had scribbled down four characters in a row: the capital letter 'I', a heart, and two neatly rendered letterforms, 'N' and 'Y'. It was so simple, something that a child could have diagrammed.

"I know this is the brief to create a logo, but I had an idea on the car ride down. The big secret of this," Glaser continued to the audience, "is replacing the verb with a noun. Change the language and make people solve the problem. The 'I' is a complete word, the heart is a symbol for an emotion, and NY are the initials for a place. So you have to figure it out. It's a puzzle that's easily solved by simply reading it. I like this, what do you think?" He paused and stood back – his pitch made quietly and succinctly -- in front of a snazzy Lichtenstein print on the conference room wall and waited.

Christian wasn't sure. "It's too abstract and cryptic. People won't get it." He liked the simplicity of the four components, but worried that people wouldn't bother to interpret it right. It wasn't complicated, but a marketing message is only as good as what its dimmest recipient takes in.

"That's the beauty of it," Glaser countered. "You feel smart when you figure it out." Glaser had been in hundreds of meetings with advertising people. They always talked too much and over others' conversations. They treated their clients like they are country bumpkins, overexplaining everything, being clever and tone deaf. Then came the Albany and city folks and their speechifying.

William Doyle laughed. "I'm just a dumb mick, but I figured it out. Reminds me of the LOVE statue in Philly. I think it's great. Let's look at it on t-shirts and show it to some real people and hear what they say."

The ads began airing in late spring and 'I Love New York' caught on quickly. Entire casts of Broadway shows and celebrities like Frank Sinatra and Liza Minelli declared their love for New York. Gas stations began selling out of New York State maps. Bumper stickers started showing up all over the city and within three months, 90% of people in target markets were aware of the campaign and the additional $28 million in tourism revenue to the State.

Suddenly, New Yorkers had rediscovered their city. The mainstream media who had foretold New York's slow death were now celebrating its apparent recovery. Even the *Los Angeles Times*, always a critic, wrote about the city's 'amazing comeback.' Travel writers reported on 'the beautifully renovated hotels and spectacular views from the new five-star restaurant atop the north tower of the World Trade Center.' There were 93,000 requests for the tourism brochure and hotel occupancy hit 90%.

New York was back.

Twenty-Five

Angie never saw it coming. She'd earned every right to be wary. Jack "Stanley" Dakota was the closest thing to a boyfriend she'd ever known and they'd been allies, never a couple. When he moved to San Francisco three years ago, Jack finally admitted he'd preferred men, which she'd known all along. They still talked, occasionally, catching up. But the rest of the lot were rats, she'd decided; in Steve's case, *über* rats. She hadn't dated since.

Her friendships sustained her; Candy, for one. Toni too. Edie had been there for her before she cracked up. And she'd known Christian for years. Lately, she noticed a bit of flirtatious chemistry simmering beneath their easy friendship. He'd always been unfailingly polite, but lately she noticed his caring, attentive side. Could this gentle and generous man be the charm?

He championed her talents, admired her grit, and gave Angie the priceless gift of feeling seen. It didn't hurt that Christian made her laugh. As they swatted *bon mots* back and forth, she found she could send him into fits of giggles, too. She'd never met anyone who took the time to earn her trust. The feeling was unfamiliar, but she wondered if it was the tenderness she'd heard others describe.

On a late April morning he called, sounding excited. "Guess what? I've got VIP tickets for this new club opening in midtown. It's tomorrow night—and I've *heard* you're into disco? Is that true, Ms. Lovejoy?"

Angie laughed. The tickets had turned up in her mailbox, too. Candy Barre was thrilled at her invitation, but she'd had to cancel. "I promised little Stevie I'd come to his birthday party. Forgot it's tomorrow. Nice aunt, right? Angie, I'm so sorry to miss going with you."

"How about *we* make it a date?" he suggested. "We'll give our extra tickets to the worst dressed sad-sacks on the sidewalk. Fashion charity begins at the velvet rope, you know."

Studio 54 was, in fact, "a dictatorship at the door, and a democracy on the dance floor," as Andy Warhol described it later. The capricious selection process could be downright cruel. But co-owner Steve Rubell compared it to mixing a salad or casting a play. He'd often stand outside on a stepstool, surveying the crowd to hand-pick the lucky ones.

Rubell and Ian Schrager met at Syracuse University. Ambitious to the point of arrogant, the pair had purchased the abandoned CBS television studio in Midtown. With little patience for city ordinances or building permits, they sank $400,000 into the space, transforming it into an oasis of disco decadence in just six weeks. When Studio 54 opened in April, 1977, they hadn't even bothered to secure a liquor license.

Christian and Angie waved their tickets at Steve Rubell, who stood outside his new club on a stepstool, surveying the crowd. When he spotted ticket holders, he'd signal the bouncer to unhook the velvet rope and let them pass through.

"It was a spectacular freak show," Angie recalled. "Shirtless busboys in white satin gym shorts or sequined jockstraps strutted like bantam roosters. The big curved bar faced a row of banquettes, covered in silver vinyl."

Above the enormous dance floor, giant spinning light tubes would drop down into the crowd. Above it, busty women hung from trapezes like plump bats while the sound system played Cheryl Lynn screaming, "Got to be Real, *It's got to be Real*'. The ceiling in back of the dance floor was rigged with a series of scrims, so the club's look and ambiance would change from one night to the next.

Steve took VIP's through a warren of storage rooms in the basement, to escape the pandemonium upstairs. Not that there was any privacy offered or desired. People came to Studio 54 to be seen and to misbehave.

On any given night, the crowd might include Halston, Truman Capote, or Bianca Jagger, who famously rode a white horse onto the dance floor, led by a man and woman who were naked, their bodies painted with circus costumes while the club's massive sound system played her husband's

'Sympathy for the Devil.' Capricious selectivity was part of the club's brand.

The President's mother, Lillian Carter reflected on her first visit. "I don't know if it's heaven or hell, but it was wonderful." Rubell and Schrager's rocket exploded when the IRS raided the club, due to another detail they'd overlooked. The jig was up. Both pled guilty to tax evasion; both served time in jail.

"I looked over toward Christian who was chatting with a big group of people, one of them looked like Reggie, with a pretty model on his arm. I walked right up to him and said 'I watched you hit a home run for the Lewiston Broncs back in '66. The ball sailed clear into my cousin's house."

His face lit up as he registered the moment. "*Wow!* I remember that day, my first professional home run. Thirteen years ago."

"You damn near knocked a window out of the house. I've still got the ball," she said. "Maybe someday I'll send it to you."

Reggie Jackson beamed an enormous smile and laughed heartily. "Thank you! You should autograph it for me."

"It was big news in town for the next week. I left not long after and moved here."

"I moved here last year," he answered, avoiding mention of the bidding war and how the Yankees had fought to get him. "I like it here."

"You should. Fifteen million people are glad you're here. And we're both out of Idaho. I'm Angie. I like it here too. It grows on you, mostly in a good way."

"This is my friend Lise Ryall," Jackson said, turning toward his date. A tall blonde woman greeted her with a smile. "We live in a very small world. Two people who lived in Lewiston Idaho dancing their cares away at Studio 54. The American Dream."

"You write good headlines."

"Just a lot of practice," he snickered, walking away with a wave and his small entourage. "You gotta be sharp in this city. Nice meeting you Angie."

"You too Reggie. My grandma still has that ball you hit in Lewiston," she said. "I'll find it and send it to you."

Reggie Jackson beamed an enormous smile and laughed heartily. "Thank you! You should autograph it for me."

Just then, the dance floor filled, and a spotlight trained on her, as the first few bars of her song played. Angie shielded her eyes. "Ladies and gentlemen," the deejay announced, "we have Angela Truelove here tonight, the composer and singer of 'Deep, Deep, Deep. Let's give it up for our disco diva!" Angie waved, stunned as the song powered up and the room moved to the beat—her beat.

As the dance crowd cheered, Reggie pointed back at her, mouthing, *That's You?* through the noise, then leaned in to give her a Major League hug followed by a high five, laughing. She scanned the room, Christian by her side. There was Sly Stallone clapping, Andy even stood up, sending her a private wink. She felt like a famous celebrity. As Angie watched the dancefloor fill, the cocaine hit. She wished the moment would last forever.

When she woke up, Angie was alone in a warm and wonderful bed, the largest and softest she'd ever known. The room was silent, filled with pillows and artwork, and as she moved under the sheets, she felt the crisp elegance of ironing. As the night before floated back into focus, she could smell coffee and bacon cooking as Peter Allen's 'The More I See You' played in the kitchen.

Quarter-'till-nine. She'd had gotten the best night of sleep she could remember and felt like she was still in a dream in a fancy hotel. Angie couldn't wait to get out of bed to see where she was ... or to stay right here until she woke up. She thought of Nana and smiled from ear to ear.

"Good morning," the door opened and Christian, looking more like an attentive waiter than the man she had slept with, walked in with a tray that included a pot of coffee, orange juice, three Tylenols and the *New York Times*. "Rise and shine. I'm a hopeless early riser and you are beautiful in the morning. Thank you!"

Angie was still foggy over the prior evening's events. She recalled Bianca Jagger riding a majestic white horse across the dance floor with her husband singing 'Sympathy to the Devil.' Angie smiled remembering 'Deep, Deep, Deep' being played and everyone dancing. Last evening at

Studio 54 would require a lot more unbundling but she had finally met her hero, Reggie. Handsome and polite, Jackson remembered Lewiston better than she did. Her head hurt too much to think any further beyond the glass of orange juice and this big, beautiful bedroom, larger than her East Village apartment.

Sex with Christian was as unexpected as breakfast in bed with him. The sex had been good and passionate, Christian had a polite intensity about him that she was surprised by. Maybe flattered by too? Christian had made a simple omelet with ham, cheese and chives with three perfectly cooked bacon rashers and an English muffin. He stood at attention, a broad smile across this face, without a hint of awkwardness. "The only thing that pulls me out of a hangover is a good breakfast and a long walk."

He climbed into bed and poured coffee. "Sugar? Cream? What do you want to do today?"

"Let's do things we've never done before."

"Like what? I grew up here. I think I've done everything ... and a few I won't admit to."

Twenty-Six

"I've never been in Tiffany's for one," Angie answered, with a smile. "I've walked by it a hundred times. And there are a few others. I've never seen a Yankees game although I'm now on a first name basis with its star player."

"Sounds like a plan," he answered. "OK, let's start at Tiffany's. It's a twenty-minute walk and I've got $25 in my wallet. I'm going to buy you a present. That's not too extravagant, is it?"

"That's very sweet. I don't know what we're going to find there for $25."

Angie and Christian walked south down Madison Avenue, as the city began to wake up. There were joggers heading for the park and unshaven men in sweat clothes carried plastic bags with bagels and cups of coffee back to their apartments. The street sweepers were out erasing the remnants of last night's festivities and fancy clothes shops were unlocking the folding security gates guarding their picture windows.

"I have to admit to never being up in time to see shops opening, so that's a first for me." They crossed at the light on 57th Street and walked west toward Fifth Avenue, entering the empty cavernous store.

A short bald smiling man greeted them at the door. "Good morning, may I help you?"

"Actually yes, thank you. We're looking for a present for the lady," Christian answered.

The sales clerk smiled, gesturing to the large glass cases that dominated the clean bright space. "Certainly sir. Was there something you had in mind?"

"Well," he answered smiling. "We had considered diamonds and—I don't want to offend you—but the lady feels that diamonds are tacky for her."

Angie jumped in. "Oh, I think diamonds are divine on *older women*, but I don't think they're right for me. I hope you understand."

"Certainly," the clerk answered with a short but puzzled smile.

"In all fairness," Christian replied. "I think I ought to explain, in addition, that there's the secondary matter of budget. Our finances this morning are…limited."

"May I ask how limited?"

"Twenty-five dollars. At the outside," Christian answered.

The sales clerk nodded. "I see. Frankly sir, the selection of merchandise at that price point is rather limited. However, I do think we might have – let me see – strictly as a novelty, you understand, for the lady and gentleman who have everything, a sterling silver telephone dialer. The cost is $24.50, including tax."

"That sounds lovely. We'll take it. Thank you so much!"

Angie threw her arms around Christian, squeezing him tight. "Didn't I tell you? This is a lovely place!"

They continued south on Madison Avenue, passing Brooks Brothers on 45th and further down on 39th, a Woolworth's. Angie grabbed his arm. "I have an idea. Let's steal something," she said. "Come on. Don't be a chicken. I've never stolen anything in my life."

Christian laughed and nodded. "Me neither. What a good plan for the day! We can look forward to a romantic dinner at Riker's Island."

"Then we can call a lawyer with our new telephone dialer."

They entered the store and saw a large table full of plastic pumpkins, black pointy witches' hats, and colorful costumes of all shapes and sizes. The saleslady was occupied with a group of nuns who were trying on masks. Angie picked up a mask from the display and slipped it over her face. She giggled and chose another, putting it on Christian. Then she took his hand, turned around and walked right out of the store. It was as simple as that. They were in and out in less than a minute.

Outside, they ran a few blocks to make their caper more exhilarating but no one from the store had noticed the laughing couple walking out in plastic dog and cat masks. Now they were strolling up Fifth Avenue, arm and arm like a couple in a Blake Edwards movie. They joined a parade of men in kilts playing 'Semper Fidelis' marching north toward the park, peeling off at 59th Street.

"You know, I've never bought a hot dog on the street before," Christian paused, noticing the dog cart with a large yellow and blue umbrella.

"Oh c'mon, really? And I thought *I* grew up in a bubble."

"Duella thought they were unsanitary and would never buy me one. Roasted chestnuts were the only street food she ever considered."

"We were told to eat meat sparingly. LDS life was arbitrarily penal. You know? Cults."

"Well, here we are," Christian nodded with a laugh. "Trying new things. Do I put the sauerkraut right on the bun? Or, is it like cole slaw?"

"You're hopeless, but we'd probably be strung up in Lewiston. Eating meat, thieving, having sex. Thank you for broadening my world."

"No, thank you Lula Mae."

They awkwardly tried to eat hot dogs leaning against a tree, hoping the mustard and sauerkraut would stay in the bun. Christian laughed. "Have you ever been up to Harlem?"

Had affection and sex finally come together for the first time in her life? Christian was a good friend. But now she craved him in an entirely new way. A secret door to an old-fashioned love story had opened and all kinds of wonderful feelings came rushing out to greet her.

Sex had always bewildered Christian. At one point growing up, he was smitten with the cool freshman girls; by his senior year he was more attracted to the football players. Christian had experimented with both during his life, but always preferred female company -- they were more interesting to talk to than men.

Over the years he'd noticed that men become self-important and repetitive in conversation, particularly if they've been drinking. They often forgot the basic give-and-take of polite conversation that women naturally embrace.

Christian continued to see Carlos off and on. He had moved to Los Angeles three years ago to pursue modeling and acting, but returned to New York several times a year to see family and friends. Carlos had become a household face—and body—posing for Calvin Klein underwear ads. He had also gotten a minor role in 'Law of Desire', Pedro Almodóvar's latest movie about the perils of fandom for gay celebrities. Carlos still made time for Christian on most trips east, but he had become a star. Everyone wanted a piece of him.

Christian considered himself bi-sexual, a category he was happy with if anyone felt compelled to bring it up. He'd grown up in simpler, more private times where sexuality wasn't discussed, just accepted and certainly not paraded. Christian had learned how to discreetly bob and weave when questions arose. Traveling abroad several times a year kept him loose and unattached. At Princeton he had a girlfriend, but they only slept together a few times when they were dead drunk. He met his first boyfriend there too, but that was more ogling than canoodling.

Over the years, Christian still enjoyed occasional clandestine one-night stands with picked-up men, but he wasn't as interested in it as when he was younger. He and Carlos still had their part time thing, now going on for close to a decade and they'd gone to Half Moon Bay last winter for a long weekend. Christian was proud of him. He was a polite, warm and grateful person who made him feel physical, even sexual.

Angie didn't particularly like Christian's ongoing relationship with Carlos, but she kept her mouth shut. She was no moral exemplar, still she wasn't sleeping around with other women. She'd met Christian and Carlos together, so he wasn't hiding anything. But sex was complicated for both of them, although Angie had mostly forsworn it. She longed for love, instead, but until now, she figured she didn't deserve it, or worse, that love would pass her by.

Twenty-Seven

Angie and Christian had been 'shacking up' as Marge put it, affectionately, in a brownstone just off Central Park West on West 76th Street. As a child, he'd ventured across Central Park with Duella to see the dinosaurs at the Museum of Natural History a few times. The Upper East Side had always been home to him. He never imagined he'd find domestic bliss on the West Side, and with a disco star from Idaho, no less.

Angie had never had anyone solidly in her corner but Ada. Now, with Christian, she felt loved unconditionally. A peaceful satisfaction settled over her for the first time in years. So, when Christian asked her to marry him in the spring of 1980, they slipped down to City Hall for a simple ceremony, then joined Marge, Isaac, Duella, and Candy for a celebratory dinner at The Odeon.

They both loved the neighborhood's bohemian vibe. The musicians, aspiring actors, and former soap stars who lived there never seemed to be in a rush. After fifteen years, she finally considered herself a New Yorker and shared the jaded exhaustion of natives, like her husband, who shrugged at most everything. New York had lost its grace and quirky neighborliness. Business had bounced back, which Angie admitted, was a good thing. But people had hardened in this new money-driven climate.

Ronald Reagan's theory of "trickle-down economics" brought a raging bull market that was accompanied by mass closings of public mental health centers across the city. Thousands of troubled people were tossed onto the street to fend for themselves. Now, an increasing number of people wandered the sidewalks mumbling to themselves, pushing shopping carts filled with their life's possessions. New York had raced back, but the roadway to the future was strewn with flat tires, blown gaskets, and burnt rubber.

Reagan insisted the private sector would save the economy. New York was hot again, but Christian's new neighborhood showed little evidence of this. Young urban professionals were moving in, spreading the news, and making a brand-new start of it. The President's gentle voice and stumbling cadence couldn't conceal the displacement of the urban flotsam who were taking up valuable space. Trade unions and civic socialism were officially dead and buried. It was Wall Street's turn to look after the city now.

Angie and Christian often took refuge at the All State Café, with a barely legible wooden sign in front. Customers descended a few steps down from the sidewalk to enter the poorly-lit space with its Select-o-Matic jukebox and small TV showing Yankee games. A subterranean outpost for actors, oddballs, and neighbors alike, they were drawn by the wonderful cheeseburgers and fried chicken.

Twenty small wooden tables engraved with initials were packed into the space. Green lanterns hung from the ceiling and plaques of sponsored Little League teams were fastened to the brick walls. It was the only bar in town where patrons could play back-to-back Steppenwolf, Ray Charles, Johnny Cash and the Zombies, while listening to the encyclopedic Frannie Mulligan opine about just about everything.

Christian met Franny years ago at Café Au Go Go. He'd moved to New York from Baltimore in the mid-sixties to go to film school at NYU, but never got around to the second semester. Franny had a wry smile and lazy left eye that made him always appear bemused. He'd bought the bar for nothing after *Looking for Mister Goodbar* came out, branding the café as a dangerous pick up joint. Franny had ruled the roost ever since. Anyone who ordered a strawberry daiquiri was turned away. He was picky about his clientele.

Franny did a bit of everything: cooking some nights, tending bar on others. He chatted up customers and wasn't above running out to the Fairway Market for a bushel of potatoes. All kinds of people were regulars: a homicide police detective, up-and-coming actors and television writers, underemployed neighbors who liked to watch *Jeopardy* in the afternoon darkness of a proper bar.

Kevin, one of the part-time bartenders, had been acting in soaps and just hit the big time with his turn in *Diner*. Now that 'The Chip,' as patrons called him, had filmed *Footloose,* his bartending days were numbered. The other bartender, Katie Bailey, was a loquacious Irish dancer with bright blue eyes and a wry expression, also looked for her place among the footlights. This happy island of cranks and fruitcakes was perfect for an aging ad man and retired pop singer.

One lazy late autumn Sunday evening a few weeks before Christmas, Detective Glenn Johnson burst through the wooden door, yelling to Katie, "Turn on the TV, turn on the TV!" as a burst of police cars, sirens blaring, streaked up 72nd Street from the West Side Highway. "John Lennon's been shot," he screamed. "Some nutcase up at the Dakota just killed him. Turn on the goddamn TV!"

Around 10:50, John Lennon and Yoko Ono had returned to their Dakota apartment building on the corner of West 72nd Street and Central Park West. They got out of the limousine, passed Mark David Chapman and walked toward the arched entrance of the building. From the street behind them, Chapman fired five hollow-point bullets from his .38 revolver, hitting Lennon in the back and shoulder. The deafening explosion left the heavy, sickly smell of gunpowder hanging in the air, as several people rushed into the courtyard to see what just happened. The city, and the world, would soon go into mourning.

Chapman tossed the gun onto the pavement and took *The Catcher in the Rye* out of his coat pocket. He took off his hat and coat and threw them onto the ground. He knew the police would come soon. "I was anxious," Chapman said later from his jail cell at Attica. "I wanted the police to hurry up and come. I was pacing and holding the book. I tried to read, but the words were crawling all over the pages. Nothing made any sense. I just wanted the police to come and take me away from there."

Mark David Chapman was a weirdo of the first order. "There were gargoyles," he remembered. "I leaned against a black rail between them. It's like I was a real gargoyle that had come to life." He looked across 72nd Street at the forbidding, Gothic-style building overlooking Central Park. Chapman was dressed warmly in long underwear, a V-shaped sweater, wool pants and a navy-blue London Fog rain coat.

His thick black hair was combed back and covered with a synthetic fur hat. It was warm for December and he had way too many clothes on. He smiled at two young women who were standing on the street corner. "Hi," he said, touching his right hand to the corner of his hat in an playful salute. "You gals are waiting for someone, I'll bet."

The shorter, blond woman replied with a sassy smile. "As a matter of fact we were waiting for you. It wasn't worth it," she added, turning her head coyly, before exploding into hysterics. She held out her hand in a gesture of friendship. "I'm sorry," she followed on, noticing the man's awkwardness. "I didn't mean to make you feel bad. We were only teasing. Let's start over. I'm Jude. Jude Stein. This is my friend Jery. Jeryl Moll."

He smiled back and took the woman's outstretched hand. "Hey Jude, don't make it bad. I'll bet nobody ever said that to you before."

The woman groaned and Chapman laughed loudly at his pun. "I heard John Lennon lives here," he continued. "I was hoping to get his autograph. I was wondering whether he might be in town." The overdressed man was plump with a sheen on his moon face, but had a friendly smile.

"You can be sure of one thing," Jude answered. "John Lennon is somewhere in New York City."

"I'm visiting from Hawaii and hoped to see him in person," Chapman continued. "I've been a Beatles fan since childhood. He's the genius behind the most famous rock band in history. I'm still betting that they get back together."

"You mean you came all the way from Hawaii," Jery asked. "Just to see John?"

"Well, I came to see John, yes," he answered. "There's more to it than that. I imagine I'll be doing more while I'm here in New York City than just seeing John Lennon."

The conversation trailed off and the three stood silently for several minutes. Finally, Jery spoke up. "Jude and I are considered family to the Lennons," she boasted. "They know our names and sometimes they come over and talk to us."

Judith Stein and Jeryl Moll had become close friends after they had met, about four years earlier, outside the Dakota. The doorman had come to consider the pair semi-permanent Dakota fixtures, standing through sun, rain and snow on many days over the past few years.

"Have you bought *Double Fantasy*?" Jude asked. ""It's his best work in years. He's got that magic again. You should go over to Tower Records on Broadway. You could buy one and maybe get it signed."

"That's a great idea," Chapman said. "Back in Hawaii they would never believe I could get John Lennon's autograph on one of his albums."

"We're going to have lunch over at the Dakota Grill. You want to join us?"

"No thanks," he answered cheerfully. "I'll be here when you get back."

When Jude and Jery returned to the Dakota at 5:15, they were surprised and disappointed to find that the gregarious Beatles fan from Hawaii had abandoned his vigil. As they turned away and prepared to head west along 72nd Street, a taxi stopped at the curb before the stone archway above the drive leading into the courtyard. A slender figure wearing a tan jacket and slouch hat opened the back door of the taxi and stepped onto the curb. John Lennon exhaled a plume of smoke from his cigarette and smiled from behind the familiar thick, circular lenses.

He greeted Jery and Jude by name. To the women's delight, he lingered to chat for several minutes about the sudden success of *Double Fantasy*. When Lennon disappeared beneath the archway, Jery said good night to her friend and headed home to Brooklyn. She wondered what had happened to the friendly man who had come from Hawaii to get Lennon's autograph.

His mind racing too fast to sleep, Mark David Chapman rose early on the morning of December 8th and began to collect his possessions that were strewn around the Sheraton hotel room. He began to neatly arrange an assortment of items he'd brought to New York and place them in an orderly semicircle on top of the hotel dresser: his passport, an eight-track tape of the music of Todd Rundgren, a small bible open to The Gospel According to John. He also left a letter from a former YMCA supervisor where he had worked with Vietnam War refugees four years earlier. Beside the letter were two photographs of himself surrounded by laughing Vietnamese children. At the center, he placed a small 'Wizard of Oz' poster of Dorothy and the Cowardly Lion.

Satisfied with the arrangement on the dresser, Chapman put on his trench coat and hat and draped a silk scarf around his neck. He stood before the full-length mirror in the room, studying the outline of the gun in his pocket. It was a .38-caliber Special Charter Arms revolver. He had torn and fitted several thick pieces of cardboard to try to conceal the obvious image of a gun in his pocket. He'd noticed that his hand got sweaty and uncomfortable when he had to keep the pistol concealed in his coat pocket for any length of time.

He slid the cardboard into his coat and smiled when he saw that it made the weapon disappear. Still watching himself in the mirror, Chapman reached into the side pocket of his suitcase and withdrew five stubby bullets. Feeling their weight in the palm of his hand, he carefully examined each one. They were hollow-point slugs, dimpled at their leaden tips to ensure that they would shatter on impact.

He inserted the cartridges into the five empty slots in the gun's cylinder. Still watching himself in the mirror, Chapman held the loaded pistol aloft in his right hand and snapped the chamber shut with a flick of his wrist. "The Catcher in the Rye of my generation," he announced to his image. "Chapter Twenty-Seven."

Chapman picked up the copy of *Double Fantasy* he's purchased yesterday and slid it snugly under his arm. He looked around the hotel room a final time, studying the items on the dresser. He hoped the collection would tell the right story that people would understand. He still needed to find a copy of *Catcher in the Rye,* but he'd noticed a B. Dalton several blocks up near Lincoln Center. They'd have copies for sure.

Chapman stepped off the elevator into the lobby of the Sheraton and walked past the checkout desk. Everything was in place as he strode north along the crowded, Monday-morning sidewalk past Columbus Circle. He spotted the bookstore up ahead on the left and entered through the revolving door. The bookstore was large, bright and empty and he was directed toward the escalator to the second floor. "It's all alphabetical," the cashier said, pointing upward. "We should have a few copies." He smiled.

He noticed the familiar red jacket with the golden letters. It was the only copy on the shelf. He took it reverently into his hands and headed downstairs to the cash register. Once outside, he eagerly took the book from the paper bag and pulled out a pen he'd taken from the hotel. Putting his foot against the rim of a webbed, yellow trash can along the sidewalk, he placed the book and *Double Fantasy* album on his knee, before pressing the nib against the inside cover page of the book.

"This is my statement," he wrote. He paused for a moment and underlined the word *This*. He signed the statement: 'Holden Caulfield' and paused again. After several moments, he added 'The Catcher in the Rye.'

Chapman stood on the sidewalk reading at random from the book, the passages that he could almost recite by heart. Near the end of the novel on page 187, he found the dialogue he was looking for:

"This fall I think you're riding for – it's a special kind of fall, a horrible kind. The man falling isn't permitted to feel or hear himself hit bottom. He just keeps falling and falling. The whole arrangement's designed for men who, at some time or other in their lives, were looking for something their own environment couldn't supply them with. Or they thought their own environment couldn't supply them with. So they gave up looking."

Chapman felt a chill of meaning as he continued to leaf through the book. On page 197 he read: "It was Monday and all, and pretty near Christmas, and all the stores were open."

"Amazing," he said to himself. "The coincidence is just amazing. A Monday. Pretty near Christmas." He stuck the new paperback into the left pocket of his trench coat, occasionally caressing it with the tips of his fingers, and began to see his purpose now with clarity. "I will become Holden Caulfield. Not that I would become crazy. That I would actually *become* Holden Caulfield."

Jude Stein was surprised to see Chapman standing in front of the Dakota when she arrived shortly before 11 a.m. Chapman waved at her and began to talk excitedly as she approached. Jude smiled at Chapman and said hello to Pat, the doorman.

"You just missed him," Chapman said. "I missed him too. I was standing here reading and had my head down like a dummy. He pulled right up and got out of a cab and walked right by me."

The doorman smiled at Jude and confirmed that Lennon had indeed just walked by moments before her arrival. "He'll be back tonight," the doorman answered.

Twenty-Eight

Christian now oversaw the Procter & Gamble account at Wells Rich Greene. He oversaw billings of over $20 million, telling the world about Sure antiperspirant, Gleem toothpaste, and Safeguard soap. His boss, Mary Wells Lawrence didn't mince words on the challenges of working for the world's leading packaged foods company. "They are a space station in their own galaxy; a world all their own, filled with converts who have been screened to weed out uninhibited, exhibitionist, mercurial traits, or anything else that might pollute their pristine environment."

Life on the space station was civilized – sensible, rational, smart enough to be interesting and full of nice square men who generally agreed with one another. There was a clear system in place with a team of marketing research priests, who could tackle any problem along the safe and sure route to success.

P&G believed that these different levels of control kept intuition and creativity on the right footing. "We are expected to escort creativity through ascending levels of

Procter up to the authorities at the top, using all the persuasion we can muster," Mary Wells told him very directly. "You also will be expected to help train Procter's young executives along the way. Most of them are overeducated, inexperienced, and opinionated. I'll pay you handsomely for your trouble. You know the new Reaganites? This is them and God help our future."

One of the immutable laws was that any Procter product had too much invested in it to be allowed to just die. If a product was given the right branding idea and the right advertising, it never would; it couldn't. Procter's Crest toothpaste was the first to contain fluoride, a real ingredient touted by the American Dental Association to fight tooth decay. Toothpastes up until that point contained sucrose and ghost ingredients that sounded healthy.

Crest's market-leading sister brand Gleem could still tout its flavor, since it never reduced the product's sugar content. So, Procter had angel and devil brands fighting one another for 'mouth space', a strange Procterism. It was a question that Christian never could wrap his head around. Sooner or later, the FDA was going to demand every mouthwash and toothpaste remove sugar and add fluoride. Until then, he was forced to sell sugar-sweetened toothpaste. End-of-rational-discussion.

The account required Christian to fly to Cincinnati every other week to wet nurse his demanding client. At 43, Christian was too old for Ira Ginsberg's shit. A native New Yorker, Ira grew up in a Hasidic family in Brooklyn, and had little patience for talk of Mortimer's, Bobby Short, or

Gracie Mansion. He graduated from Brandeis and Columbia Business School. He was in a hurry, and tired of smug WASPs in his way. Ira Ginsberg was the client. He wasn't going to go easy on the likes of Christian.

As a child, Ira recalled walking along 47th Street in Manhattan to visit his uncle's stall in the diamond district. Along the way, the snappily-dressed Madison Avenue bull shitters with their sunglasses, cleverness and cigarettes looked him up and down in his black brimmed hat, black coat, and curls. He heard their snickers. The humiliation had lodged in his soul, never leaving him. Ira Ginsburg was still seething.

He had punched his ticket to escape the life of a medieval merchant, starting in Boston, returning to New York for graduate school at Columbia. Then he was off to Cincinnati, a provincial but necessary stop in his marketing career. He was determined to succeed in the white-bread world. He knew exactly who he was dealing with.

Ira's mornings began just after six, with a four-mile run near his new townhome in Shaker Heights before arriving at P&G at 8 a.m. sharp. He structured his day around the concept of IAM, insightful account management, in P&G parlance, a skill he expected others to follow. He'd shed his black hat, cut his curls, and discarded his orthodox traditions, before leaving for Boston, but maintained a close-cropped beard that aged him by 20 years, perhaps explaining why he remained single. A natty dresser with a slight build, he preferred tab collar shirts and Perry Ellis ties. Ira was fussy, bouncing around when he talked, whether in his condescending sing-song or, more often, barking orders.

When Ira wasn't tossing around corporate acronyms like CIB ('customer is boss') or FMOT ('first moment of truth'), he talked in complete paragraphs and insisted on 'daily catch ups' (or DCU's) with Christian, scheduled after his 5:30 internal team meetings had finished for the day. "I hope that's OK?"

It wasn't. Cocktail hour was cocktail hour after all. He had tried foisting Ira onto the account supervisor, but Ira wanted no part of that nonsense. He knew the game: He was paying prime dollar and worked for the world's best packaged food company. As a result, he sized up Christian and insisted this preppy *bon vivant* indulge his every whim.

In the span of one year, Ira had drained Christian's energy and crushed his spirit. He was focused on processes and busy work output that he learned at 'b-school' – call reports, meeting reports, follow-up memos, and daily conversations about planning the next meetings. He kept them in neatly labeled binders, carefully arranged by date. He called at inconvenient times to make last minute demands.

"My calendar is filling up fast! I'll be in the city this weekend visiting family. I'd like to come by the agency on Friday afternoon to look at a draft of the Prell media plan. And when is that new research coming back on likely Gleem users? Maybe you could organize the team for a meeting on Monday morning? I like using my time wisely." He was beyond exhausting and cocky, often addressing Christian as 'Hey Chris' before launching into his demands, always positioned as requests.

P&G was full of box checkers, fulfilling their career marches onward by being assistant product managers of Sure deodorant soap or Cheer laundry detergent. This was the nineteen-eighties with a completely new generation of clients. They deserved people their own age. Christian remembered a senior account guy named Brendan Ryan wearing a tee shirt saying, 'Turning 40. Too old to boogie, too young to die." Christian de Graaf was boogied out.

The ad business had become more like banking and law. *Process, cover your ass, process.* The eager beavers fresh out of Kellogg and Wharton were entitled, not sold on charm, hope, naughtiness, and creativity. They talked about 'delivering solutions' and liked to draw maps with lots of arrows to explain things. Their jargon was as impenetrable as their arrogance. Things had changed since Christian could make a few calls and stage the Harlem Cultural Festival or market a hit record on the back of a children's cereal box.

No one sent memos about memos or had meetings to plan future meetings, until now. He was cooked. *Get me off the grill before I'm charred.* But at least his personal life had finally settled down.

Christian stood at his office window as the wet snow thumped against the glass. The forecast was calling for a foot of the stuff. Mandi had already hurried home to Massapequa, leaving a note on his desk: *Call Ira Ginsberg this afternoon. He wants to set up a call to discuss FY82 team goals and the new campaign for Gleem. Sorry—getting out before roads get slick.*

Already, the snow was sticking to the streets below. If he didn't leave soon, his 45-minute walk home through Central Park would require a pair of snowshoes. More than a year ago, he'd met privately with Mary Wells to discuss his plans to retire, promising to stay on for six months while they searched for a replacement. "But *how* will we *ever* replace you?" she said, a persuasive technique he'd used himself. By the time he left her office, he'd caved. Wells insisted he extend his already-generous notice to 18 months.

The search for his replacement brought a parade of 'not quite right' candidates through the agency's HR department. With just weeks left on the clock, they'd managed to reel in a young Turk from N.W. Ayer. At 30-years-old, Jason Turnbull claimed to have P&G account experience, so he'd played hardball, holding out for a preposterous salary far beyond anything Christian ever made.

Still, it was worth it. If he never saw Ira Ginsberg's face or uttered another Procter & Gamble corporate acronym, it would be too soon. Life was too short to put up with clients who pushed his buttons for sport.

Wells stuck her head in his office, smiling. "He signed the contract; he'll be perfect." She caught herself. "I mean, he's no *Christian DeGraaf*. But he did help dream up the Folgers' "Wake Up" campaign. I'll leave his resume with you, if you'd like to take a look." She placed the oversized black case on the coffee table in his office. Hours later, when Christian got around to flipping through Turnbull's pages of ads, neatly inserted into plastic sleeves, he almost felt sorry for the guy.

"You're right," he told Wells, as he returned the portfolio in her office. "You picked a winner." As he tramped home through the snowy park, he felt liberated. 'Two peas in a pod,' he thought. 'He and Ira will get along famously.'

Procter & Gamble set the standard in the packaged foods world for controlled, scientific marketing – religious consumer research, self-discipline, relentless will, and staying power. Each executive was viewed as an atomic part of a huge omniscient power who demanded their ad agencies work scientifically and maturely. Their Byzantine organizational structure created layers of management, each assuring that campaigns were not only 'on-strategy,' but that each word, each nuance, no matter how small was 'Proctercorrect.'

P&G believed that these different levels of control kept intuition and creativity on the right footing. "We are expected to escort creativity through ascending levels of Procter up to the authorities at the top, using all the persuasion we can muster," Mary Wells told him very directly. "You also will be expected to help train Procter's young executives along the way. I'll pay you handsomely for your trouble. You know the new Reaganites? This is them and God help our future."

He'd had a good run, but the ad game has been drained of its spirited fun, especially for anyone over forty. The colorful characters and big names-on-the-door were cashing out, replaced by analytical types who talked about 'metrics,' 'synergies', 'whole eggs', and 'orchestration.' 'Nerds with words!' he thought. Clients now wanted agencies to handle PR, direct mail, logo design, even retail design to align chain stores in malls with the brand's message. Agencies were becoming one-stop-shops in an arid landscape where marketing-speak like ROI—return on investment—ruled the day.

Corporate cost cutters sugar coated this unpleasantness with phrases like *headcount consolidation*. Memorable campaigns like Merrill Lynch's Wall Street bull run, were too daring, too expensive. Clients demanded positive messaging only, which left precious little leeway for Mikey to eye a bowl of Life cereal with suspicion. If the layered corporate approval process didn't wring the last drop of wit, charm, or mischief from his concepts, focus groups would further dilute his ideas to weak tea.

Any hint of inefficiency was taboo to the fiscal watchdogs in accounting, a backlash from the era of sloppy leisure suits, welfare spending, and urban malaise. Christian always knew he'd leave the business once ad agencies started behaving like law firms or investment banks. With creativity and cleverness losing out to marketing jargon and cheesy slogans, what was the point?

Martin Sorrell, the prickly English number cruncher who helped build Saatchi & Saatchi's empire had left to launch his own company, naming it WPP, a dreary acronym for the even drearier Wire and Plastic Products. Martin and Ira deserved one another. They could brand the future without him.

Still, he'd always counted on working full-time well into his sixties. Seeing his ideas become full-throated campaigns brought a sense of satisfaction. The job was always more than a paycheck. Lately, he'd caught himself daydreaming of doing whatever the hell he wanted. John Lennon's assassination was the final straw. The man was only 42, for God's sake, with a wife and young child. He'd been shaken by the proximity, too. The Dakota was only a few blocks from his apartment.

Christian was 43 now, happily married to a woman he loved. It was high time they fixed up the house in Vermont. They'd still live in New York, but on their own terms, spending Sunday nights at the Lone Star Café, catching James Brown or NRBQ instead of a red eye out of LaGuardia. No more fretting over the F'83 Gleem media plan. Life's way too short to stress over sugary toothpaste, for God's sake.

Then there was the matter of Vermont. Isaac had ordered the A-frame from Sears and Roebuck. The kit came with a set of simple architectural plans and the shingles, nails, and lumber needed to build it. Neither Isaac nor Christian possessed a single handyman skill. The chalet was built exactly as specified, no upgrades.

In Isaac's opinion, copper pipes and insulation were luxuries. The wood stove sufficed, but anyone anticipating a cozy ski weekend in Stowe was in for a rude awakening. Thrifty discomfort was a core human value to Isaac, like freedom or democracy. Meanwhile, he rattled on about OPEC and the 'god-damn ragheads.'

Marge largely ignored her husband's spartan views, a coping strategy that brought the unintended consequence of saving their marriage. She left Christian and Isaac at the chalet to discuss wood rot, roof flashing, heat pumps, problems that neither had the know-how to solve, and checked herself into the nearby Trapp Family Lodge where Oscar, her favorite barman, made a bracing Beefeater martini.

Christian's parents were drawn to Vermont each fall when the leaves turned. They'd drive the back roads, avoiding the throngs of leaf peepers, marveling at the crisp air and the trees ablaze with color. Now that they'd reached their early seventies, they preferred staying put in Manhattan or visiting friends in Florida. Their distaste for its strip malls and drug lords, was overridden by their desire to escape winter in the city.

As New York continued to splinter and segregate, Christian and Angie toyed with the idea of living at Stowe year-round. Instead, they'd agreed to keep the apartment on West 76th Street, even though Angie spent far less time there. She joined Christian every few months for the drive back to the city, but Stowe's outdoor pleasures soothed a long-forgotten corner of her soul. She slept with the windows open, walked barefoot over grass and gravel, relished the quiet, and soaked up the mountains, majestic and unpredictable.

On this particular Tuesday morning, Christian kissed Angie before leaving for the city to see Carlos, in town for a photo shoot. He stayed in one of the nicer hotels in Midtown on Sixth Avenue, even when he planned to see

Christian, but their friendship had endured for almost two decades. Christian felt a swell of pride whenever Carlos landed a prestigious gig. He'd recently been cast in a Pedro Almodóvar movie which garnered decent reviews.

Carlos' charm lay in his easygoing modesty. He smiled easily and quickly, he was good with names, and when people recognized him on the street, he'd happily pose for a photo or two with them. He knew precisely how to smile, and when, so the camera caught the twinkle in his eye. Even during the high-wattage excitement of Fashion Week, he visited with his family whenever he was in town from L.A., arriving with ample presents for his preteen cousins.

Over dinner at the River Café over in Brooklyn, Carlos announced that he'd be heading to Fire Island for a few days. "C'mon, It'll be fun. We haven't gone out there in a while."

"Are you fucking nuts?" Christian erupted. "Fire Island is fuck island. You know that! How could you not be concerned? I forbid you to go there." Christian had been reading about this new 'gay cancer' that had infected upwards of 100 men in New York and San Francisco. "People are dropping like flies. *Gay men*, all of them."

"You're making a big deal out of nothing," Carlos said. They'd been out to Fire Island a few times over the years. It's always fun, but there was a frenzied desperation about the place. "I'll watch myself and stay away from the crazies. I promise."

He was a married man for heaven's sake, too old for the hurly-burly of screwing around with young bucks. Gay men could be reckless, and the long-closeted ones entered the scene ravenous, desperate to make up for lost years.

"Fuck off Christian, you're in a make-believe marriage and you're a joke cheating on your wife with a part-time boyfriend."

Christian's face reddened. "This isn't the clap, Carlos. A shot of penicillin won't cut it. It's spreading and they don't know what's causing it."

"It's not like I'm sleeping around," Carlos replied angrily. "We've talked about Titus. You'd like him. He works for William Morris, a little older than me."

"And who is *he* sleeping with?"

"I haven't had a chance to ask," Carlos answered sharply. "I've been on the road."

The conversation was going nowhere. Carlos never marched to the gay motto of *so many men, so little time*, but he had a steady companion in LA, a model. For years, he and Christian had created their own version of monogamy, even as many in this gay world found this bourgeois and trivial.

"You have a wife," Carlos noted. "What gives you the right to write the rules?" Hadn't the three of them met in Kingston back in 1975? The relationship was bound to be unconventional. "Look," Carlos said, "I know all the warning signs: night sweats, fevers, weight loss, diarrhea, tongue sores, bruises that won't heal. I have none of the above. Hell, I don't even eat Asian food anymore, because it shot my bowels for a day after. It's not like I'm cruising for single men. Never have. You know that."

"I didn't mean to accuse you of being promiscuous," Christian answered. "We've been together for a long time with few rules."

"Exactly," Carlos answered quickly. "This is about trust. Remember, it's a two-way street."

His answer was testy, signaling it was time to move on and not talk about this new disease. There were articles about a few people coming down with it through blood transfusions, so it wasn't strictly a gay affliction. Condoms were encouraged, but gay men were resistant to what that signaled about trust, fidelity and relationships. It was quipped that gay men have as much use for condoms as they do tampons.

No one could make sense of this disease, but it was ugly and spreading quickly. They held each other tight and slept together that night. It wasn't like the old days, but they still had a fifteen-year relationship.

Twenty-Nine

Angie had been dreading this moment, ever since Ada slipped and fell on some ice last winter. She had been healing slower than everyone expected and just seemed checked-out -- her spirit had gone with the fall. Over the past ten years, they talked on the phone at least once a month, but the calls had gotten more irregular and downbeat. She was tired of living … and living in Lewiston. Nothing ever really happened and everyone was only concerned about fitting in and not rocking the boat.

Ada's last gesture was to pay for her great-granddaughter's college education, provided it wasn't at BYU. That had stirred up Angie's parents but no one wanted to take on Ada, and certainly not her son. Angie never really completely fessed up to her about the porno movies, although the crack about Holly Golightly had come true, Angie had to chuckle. They had talked and laughed about Andy's oddball movies many times and she always remarked how proud she was that her favorite granddaughter 'made it' in New York after 'some experimentation.'

Ada's heart warmed as Angie told her all about marrying Christian. He made her laugh and respected her independence. What else mattered? She watched for his ads on TV, delighted to find a connection to the action in the big city. "And Nana," Angie added, "guess who I met at Studio 54?"

"Is that the famous disco? Didn't Miss Lillian go there? Who'd you meet?"

"That's the one. I also saw Reggie Jackson there. I told him about his homerun ball. And Nana? My song came on while we were talking, and when he realized that was me, he gave me a big high-five."

"Tell your friend Reggie I've kept that ball. If he promises us an autograph, we'll send it to him."

But Ada's calls came less often, lately. Angie wondered if the fall had broken Ada's spirit, too. Was she tired of living? Or just tired of living in Lewiston? In her final gesture of goodwill, Ada offered to pay Clara's college tuition, with one caveat; she could choose any college except Brigham Young. Now a senior at Boise State, it was Clara who called Angie with the news. Ada had passed peacefully in her sleep.

Angie had lost her staunchest supporter. Now she'd pay it forward, like Ada wanted. "I'll fly into Boise," she told Clara, "rent a car at the airport and pick you up at school. We can drive to Lewiston together." She looked forward to meeting Clara. Ada said they looked alike. What else would they find in common?

The last time Angie rented a car, it was the brown Vega she and Candy had taken to Teaneck to unmask Steve Caputo. When her song hit, she took a delicious pride, knowing Steve would hear it on the radio as he scrambled for work, an outcast. At the airport, the rental car company produced a shiny bronze 1980 Chevy Citation that was as awful to drive as it was to behold. A 'sporty' hatchback, she doubted the car had the horsepower to manage the route through Seven Devils Mountains and Hells Canyon.

Clara was waiting in front when she pulled up to her dorm. She bounded toward the car, waving, her own spitting image, rangy with broad shoulders, freckles, and wild curly hair. Barefoot, she wore a jean skirt and white tee shirt, a gray backpack slung over one shoulder. She turned to shout goodbye to two friends, then approached the car. "*Damn,* I *do* look like you," she laughed. "Nana always said so. And Nana's always right."

Angie smiled and gave her niece an extra squeeze as they stood, taking each other in. "You are far prettier and I gather, far sweeter, than me. I've been looking forward to this day for years," she told Clara.

"Me too. And I'm not all that sweet; Nana said I'm feisty, like you." Clara's smile was playful; she had big blue eyes and more than a few piercings, including a silver stud in her septum. She tossed her backpack into the back seat and opened the passenger door, which squeaked on its hinges. "I'll warn you," Angie said. "This tin can is no Cadillac. I've tried to get comfortable, but it's useless."

They hit it off like old friends. "Are you ready for this?" Clara asked as they headed north. She grew up hearing stories of her crazy immoral aunt, but Ada had set her straight.

"I'm ready," Angie said. "Nana is up there, directing the outcome."

"So now we're religious?"

"Damn straight. We'll need all the help we can get."

When she'd come home from college with piercings after freshman year, Clara's mother asked if the stud on the side of her nose was a booger. *"Twice!"* Clara said, sending them both into fits of laughter. Clara wanted to know all about the Jamaica recording session, her work with Warhol, and the porno movie world. The empty highway freed them to talk for hours, nothing off limits.

The long vistas and mesas hadn't changed much, but Angie noticed mini-malls with gas stations along the highway and, every so often, they'd pass cookie-cutter ranch homes in new developments with names like Shoshone Estates and Mesa Meadows, all dwarfed by the vast landscape. She'd missed Idaho's wide open spaces. "It's good to see new blood moving in," she told Clara.

Angie was heading toward family connections, long severed. She'd stay two nights, tops. They'd check into the El Rancho Motel over on North Third Street, suitably anonymous, then deal with the family tomorrow. Clara's presence steadied her. She'd have one ally, at least.

Clara's own homecomings had dwindled to the essential holidays. She'd spent the last two summers working for the U.S. Department of Agriculture in a park outside Coeur d'Alene. "Growing up, I heard all the stories…." Clara began. "Something about an affair with a baseball player? Nana said it was all bullshit."

"I was twenty-one. I thought he was my boyfriend, but Jared Bingham took that to mean he could help himself. We didn't have the term 'date rape' back then, but that's what it was. Ada believed me. And no, I never slept with Reggie Jackson. That was hogwash. *Really?* Funny, but I did meet him a few years ago. Nice guy. I owe him a baseball."

Clara had pulled out a notebook and pen along the drive north. She'd been asked to speak at the memorial service and now, feet on the console, she was working on a eulogy for her great-grandmother. They rode in silence for the last stretch, before Angie took the exit to Lewiston, and headed for the motel.

At $69 a night, the El Rancho was as charmless as it sounded. They checked in, dropped their bags, and headed to El Sombrero. The restaurant's margaritas there were 'best in town,' the hotel manager assured them. "I'd come here in high school, with my friend Gina," Clara whispered conspiratorially, once they'd been seated. "Her father owns the place. He'd give us baskets of chips and salsa after school and Coca-Colas. We'd sneak a beer out of the walk-in, sometimes, but Mr. Costa kept a close eye on the inventory."

Rafael Costa came to their table and greeted Clara warmly. Gina was off to Seattle to work for a computer company called Microsoft, whatever the hell that was. "I was sorry to hear about your grandmother," he told Clara and Angie. "She was a force for good in this community. She too enjoyed tequila," he broke into a big smile. "Quietly, of course."

A cheerful wiry man, Rafael had opened a lunch cafe in the late sixties and grown it into one of Lewiston's most popular restaurants. Locals and tourists in-the-know all raved about the place. The Costas moved into the valley fifteen years ago. "I never knew food could have, you know, *flavor?*" Clara said. The restaurant became a respite from the bland Mormon beef stroganoff, funeral potatoes, and Jell-O salad. "Prison food. Until this place opened, I didn't know anything else."

Clara ordered chili rellenos, a favorite since high school. "And could we please order a round of tequila? I'm 21 now, Mr. Costa," who nodded; Gina was, too. "My aunt Angie would like the beef tacos with your special sauce. She's treating."

"Save room for my wife's *tres leches* cake, Clara," Rafael added. "It's a recipe from her grandmother's family."

A tequila shot in a Mexican restaurant was unthinkable twenty years ago. Angie was happy to see that had changed. Nobody expected them until the next morning, so the afternoon and evening were theirs to share. Angie looked around the dining room. "You're safe here," Clara said. "Nobody else in the family likes Mexican. More green Jell-O for them," she smiled.

"So where to next year?" Angie asked. "Forestry? The sugar maples in Vermont are beautiful in the fall. You could stay in our cottage up in Stowe. The mountains are closer and the skiing is better."

Clara smiled. "Nana suggested that. I'm sold, don't worry. I don't know if I could handle New York City, but the Green Mountains look pretty sweet."

"Christian and I spend more time there, now that he's retired," Angie told her. "He's taken up carpentry, with dubious results. You'll like him. He's witty and kind, but completely useless with his hands."

Ada Lovejoy had insisted her service would take place in the courtyard of Mr. Malcolm's Brower-Wann Funeral home, rather than the LDS church on Preston Avenue. Angie nudged Clara, "she's looking down from heaven right now, loving the sight of us all gathering in this Godless place." Angie spotted her father and mother, older and plainer, standing together, silent and expressionless. American Gothic without the pitchfork.

"Hello Muddah, hello Fadduh," Angie said, approaching her parents with a goofy Allan Sherman voice that she knew would confuse them. They looked at her with an awkward curiosity. Her mother forced a smile while Jacob Lovejoy looked at the ground and fumbled in the pocket of his sport coat. Even now, the man didn't have the good sense to wear proper shoes to a funeral.

"Nice of you to be here, Angela," her mother said slowly. Her father added that she looked well, then looked away, his Adam's apple dropping down into his shirt collar. The navy sport coat and striped tie hung loosely on his bony physique; and his shirt collar gaped around his neck.

"Pretty snazzy shoes you got there Dad—Nikes?" Angie said, pointing to his feet. "They're named for the Greek goddess of victory. Very special."

Jacob smiled. "You like 'em? They're really light and dressy." He thought Nike rhymed bike. But if his wayward daughter found them snazzy, that was something.

"They look good on you Dad. You know what?" Angie asked. "I'm married now. My husband's name is Christian. So now I'm Angie de Graaf."

"When did you marry?" he asked flatly. "I guess I should say congratulations, first. Sounds like you've got a fancy new name."

"We went down to City Hall and got married, maybe three or four years ago. It's worked out great. I love him."

Jacob looked intently at his daughter as she spoke, nodding and swallowing. "That's nice. Is he here with you?"

"No dad, he's got parents to take care of in New York."

"He sounds like a nice boy."

As the recorded organ music began, the assembled group moved to take their seats in the folding metal chairs. "At the request of Mrs. Lovejoy," Mr. Malcolm announced, "we'll have a simple, non-denominational celebration of her life. She wanted it short and snappy." He smiled as several attendees whispered to one another, shaking their heads. "So we'll begin with a few remarks from her great granddaughter—Clara?"

Clara stepped forward, thanking Mr. Malcom. She wore a dark navy dress, metal nose stud in place. She looked out at the assembled group and exhaled with a nervous smile. "Nana always talked to me about dreams," she began. "She said the world needed dreamers, but it also needed doers. Above all, the world needs *dreamers that do*." She stared at her parents, seated on the fourth row. Her great uncle Jacob seemed to be fiddling with a scrap of paper in his hands.

"She loved this passage from 'Breakfast at Tiffany's.' We saw the movie together. She loved Holly Golightly, but she really loved the book by Truman Capote, even more than the movie. The passage went like this:

'Dreams start us walking down the road.
Every day, we walk a little further; a mile maybe,
Then we come home.
The next day, we walk maybe two miles,
and then come home.
Then one day, we just keep walking.'"

The stone-faced crowd puzzled over this one. If you've got a truck, or a car, why walk two miles down the road?

Here was proof: anyone who left Lewiston always came back talking gibberish. Clara continued.

"Nana used to say that a man is not old until regrets take the place of his dreams. She always told me that our actions must be louder than our words and our dreams bigger than our fears. That makes me get up every day. Thank you, Nana."

Angie's parents narrowed their eyes, trying to make sense of this. "Rest easy, sweet Nana. You left the world better than you found it. You remain a life force and I love you fiercely. May you rest in peace." Clara wiped tears from her eyes, turned away from the podium, and returned to her chair in the courtyard.

As her eldest son, Jacob Lovejoy felt duty-bound to say a few words, but his relationship with his mother had never been easy. He approached the lectern, tentative, unfolding the small scrap of paper in his hands. "I wanted to say a few words about my mother," he began mumbling, then he halted, and took the coward's way out. "Heavenly Father, we come together today to mourn the passing of our beloved family member…Grant us peace in this time of grief, and help us remember that death is not an end, but a beginning."

He looked up from his paper, folded it neatly and put it in his pocket. He moved to step away from the lectern, then stopped to add a footnote: "My mother and I didn't see eye to eye on much of anything. But she lived life on her own terms and God bless her for that." He nodded, satisfied with this feeble effort, and returned to his seat.

After a few more moments of excruciating silence, Kermit Malcom spoke up. "Unless anyone has anything else to share, that concludes our service. Mrs. Lovejoy wanted it to be a simple one. Have a nice day."

Angie noticed Jared, now a swollen middle-aged man in an ill-fitting gray suit and Vuarnets. He was talking to her older cousin. As he turned to head toward his truck, Angie approached him. "Leaving so soon?" she teased. "Wow, I thought we'd catch up on old times. How long's it been since you raped me?"

"I didn't *rape* you; you crazy bitch," he hissed under his breath, looking around to see who was in earshot. Time had done Jared no favors. His face was florid and full, flushed with sweat; even his thinning hair was dampened.

"Yeah. But here's the thing, Jared. You did," she answered, staring at him. "And you ran me out of town." She paused, watching him snarl as his youngest daughter ran up to grab his leg. "Aren't you going to introduce us?" He shot her a look filled with arrogant rage.

"Hi, I'm Angie," she said to the little girl, sweetly. "Your dad and I grew up together." She bent at the waist and extended her hand as Jared shouted to his brood.

"C'mon you all. We gotta go, *now*." Mrs. Bingham was nowhere in evidence. The youngest fell in line, but the two older ones were running amok down the sidewalk. "*Joshua! Rebecca!!* I said *now!*" As Jared Bingham walked his sextet of blonde children toward the dull, dented Ford Ranger parked across the street, Angie smiled and waved, as if they were old chums. Clearly, she'd gotten under his thin skin.

She turned to approach her parents. Her mother had spilled tomato juice on the front of her white dress; she was fussing with a napkin, trying to blot the stain. "You all right Mom?" she asked. "You seem unsettled."

She glanced up toward her daughter. "I'm fine," she answered impatiently. "But I'm worried about your father. He's pretty shook up about Nana. He's mad at himself, too. He called her a witch to her face. That was his last word to her."

"Are you sure he said *witch?*" she asked her mother, gently. "Or did the word *rhyme* with witch?" Her mother turned away, wiping a tear from her face.

"No, Angela. He said witch. Your father would never use profanity, particularly to his mother. He just wouldn't say something like that."

"Is that true Dad?" Angie asked. "You called Nana a bitch? Were those your last words to her? *Whew*, that'll get you a ticket to purgatory. Boy, you must feel awful! I'm so sorry to hear that, Dad." Then she turned and walked over to Clara, who had attracted a group of young admirers. Clara was cool. They got her message: *get the hell out of Lewiston as soon as they could.*

They asked her about Boise State and what she planned to do after graduation. They'd heard about her working up in the Bitterroots. What was that like? She was home so rarely, Thanksgiving and Christmas, and they were bursting with questions about what she'd seen, who she'd met, and where she'd been.

Angie was pleasantly surprised. She knew the old guard wouldn't care much for her. Given her 'love child' with Reggie, she could hardly blame them. But the younger nieces and cousins all asked her about New York City, about Blondie, and Andy, and her song, *they loved her song.* What was it like, they all wanted to know, to get into Studio 54?

Thirty

Carlos was gone before dawn, leaving Christian feeling untethered. Their argument had fueled a deepening dread and his early morning walk through the Upper West Side had done nothing to clear his head. This new disease scared the hell out of him. They'd danced around it far too long, but now that they'd talked, Christian only felt worse.

By 1981, doctors in California and New York had diagnosed 41 cases of a rare, often fatal form of cancer turning up in gay men. The medical world was baffled. They saw no evidence of contagion, but the cancer was spreading like wildfire, 'outing' legions of closeted men, from Rock Hudson and Roy Cohn to Brady-Bunch dad, Robert Reed.

Blood transfusions turned up as the source of a few cases. Maybe this wasn't a strictly gay disease? Condoms were encouraged, but for gay men, a condom signaled mistrust, despite the ugly disease that kept spreading.

They ended the fight with sex, a wrongheaded game of Russian roulette to prove their fidelity. Now Carlos was on a train bound for Fire Island, a cesspool of clueless queens looking to fuck whoever was game. The recklessness of this decision left Christian fuming. He missed Angie.

She called later that morning from the airport in Boise. "Don't wait up," she told him. She'd land at LaGuardia that night, but her flight was delayed. "I'll be fine taking a cab." She'd dreaded the trip home to Idaho. Not the funeral. Just her family. Christian was glad Clara had joined her. They'd decided to head for Stowe in the morning. The mountains would do them both good.

As dusk fell, he punched a button on the microwave to reheat leftovers from Hunan Cottage and poured himself a glass of wine. It didn't help. He couldn't shake the image of Carlos on Fire Island.

As he picked at his food, Christian flipped through the day's mail. The estimate for the new septic field had arrived. You'd think Isaac owned a camper van, not a house. He'd seriously considered an outhouse years ago, just to avoid the cost of installing a septic system. "Why not over there?" he'd grumbled, pointing to a spot in the yard on an upward slope.

Christian reminded the Dutch Master that The Great Depression was over. It was time to bite the bullet and spend the money to shore up the chalet. But Isaac wasn't having it. "Tell you what," Christian backpedaled. "We'll split the cost. Angie and I spend half the year there. We'll pay our share. Would that help?" He would inherit the chalet eventually. Might as well start budgeting for it.

Marge had lost interest in Vermont's rustic charms. The deGraafs had simplified their lives, preferring to shuttle between New York and Florida. Isaac still griped about the price of absolutely everything but Marge had learned to tune out his money talk. Four years of steady market upticks under Ronald Reagan had done little to dispel Isaac's belief that a stock market crash was imminent. "A mortgage-backed security?" he grumbled. "That's not even real; they're selling funny money."

Christian loaded the car and they set out before dawn to avoid the tunnel traffic. Once they'd eased onto the highway, Angie emerged from her sleepy fog, ready to talk. "Did I tell you Clara's thinking of moving to Manchester? She wants to go into forestry after graduation, so I was pushing Vermont. Why not? I'd love to have her close by." Then she shifted gears, "How's Carlos? You said he was in town."

"He's fine," Christian answered. "We had dinner on Friday. Then he headed out to Long Island to see friends."

Angie shot Christian a pained look. "We've talked about this, Christian. You know it's spreading. They're calling this thing an epidemic now. Is everyone being careful?"

"Yes," Christian snapped. "He's taking the proper precautions."

"And you?" she asked sharply. "From what I read, I have the right to ask. When sex is involved, it's my business, too."

"We're both being careful," he said, eager to change the subject. "Tell me about Idaho."

"Strange as expected," she said vaguely. "My parents couldn't look me in the eye. It's so sad. But Clara found my letters in Ada's closet. She kept them, all of them, in a shoebox. I can't wait to re-read them."

Christian's answer did little to satisfy Angie. Doctors were reporting swollen lymph nodes and violet spots, like bruises, emerging as the disease ravaged the body. Some cases were traced to blood transfusions but until the CDC knew more, everyone needed to be careful. People were rationalizing risky behaviors, just to cope with the fear. "I'm married," he reasoned. "It isn't like I'm screwing around. I see Carlos only a few times a year."

"Just use a goddamn condom," Angie snapped. "Don't fuck around with this disease. I learned that lesson the hard way, remember?" For Angie, a condom was as much of a part of having sex as buckling up to drive a car. Aside from her fear of pregnancy and STDs, she believed sex was sex; keep the fluids and emotions out of it. Even with Christian, Angie hadn't had unprotected sex since her Studio 54 days. "Easier to clean up." Spooning was far more romantic anyway.

They rode in silence until, at last, the rutted gravel driveway came into view. Mud season had passed, and their collective mood brightened as the house emerged through the leafy trees. After a June wedding in New York, they would stay the summer, flinging open the windows to enjoy the cool breezes and hear the birds.

Christian had lined up a contractor to inspect the roof and replace a few wood-rotted windows. They'd meet him tomorrow. "What about that deck off the kitchen?" he asked in a bid to regain her favor. "Let's get him to run an estimate." It was high time they added a spot to admire the view.

Three days later, Marge rang Christian. Isaac had dropped dead at his desk, she told him. When she found him slumped over, he'd been gone for an hour or more working, as always. Given that Isaac never exercised a day in his life and still smoked two packs of Camels a day, he'd been lucky to reach 76. But for Christian, his father's death hit hard.

"I've never heard her sound so shaky," he told Angie as they made the drive back to New York that evening. After nearly 40 years of marriage, Marge and Isaac had settled into a comfortable affection, a WASP détente. She was the personality, driving the social bus; he was the straight man. He'd dabble in her parties but was happiest alone in his study, managing his investments and reading policy papers and public bankruptcy laws for the sheer pleasure of it.

Once they'd dispatched the question of law school, Christian and his father had cultivated a mutual admiration, rarely exchanging cross words. Isaac never hinted at disapproving remarks about his son's sexual proclivities. And the stern scarecrow with a brain had quietly made New York City a better place to live, and Christian loved him for that.

After Isaac's service, Angie took the car to Vermont to meet the contractor while Christian remained in New York. He'd need a couple of days to meet with the family's estate lawyer, collect copies of Isaac's death certificate, and see that Marge got settled. He'd head up to Vermont on Thursday.

"We need to fix that gaping hole under the eave," Angie said over the phone after the contractor left. He'd found Stowe's squirrel population holed up in the attic, along with a carpet of black walnuts two inches deep. The contractor had traced the entry point to several rotten boards. "He said we'll have Noah's Ark up there if we don't do something about it soon," she chuckled. Maybe Isaac would finally be paying for the repairs after all?

Isaac had refused to replace the roof a decade ago, after a builder had quoted him $15,000. "We'll soldier through," he loved saying. "But it's too goddamned expensive. It cost me half that to build the place." His pennywise, pound-foolish arguments about lowering the thermostat, as heat and money escaped through the roof oddly never registered with the Dutch Master.

"Could I come by to pay my respects to your mother?" Carlos was back in New York for Fashion Week. "Or would a note be better?" Marge may have been grieving, but Carlos' juicy gossip about LA life never failed to perk her up. "I'd love to see you," he added. "I understand if too much is going on, but I've always loved your parents. They were so open-minded when no one else was."

"Of course," Christian answered. He was worried about his mother. Carlos would be a comfort to them both. He'd never seen Large Marge act fragile but she'd been holed up in her bedroom, avoiding calls and visitors. "I'll be here for a few days, then I'm headed back up to Vermont. We're finally renovating the chateau. *Ooh la la."*

Christian showed up at Melon's half drunk. Through most of their dinner, his eyes welled with tears. Isaac was a good man, he and Carlos agreed. New Yorkers would miss him, even those who never knew him. Christian recounted his behind-the-scenes heroics, sparing the city from the perils that the public never knew.

Then he turned to the Harlem Nights concert, Isaac's gift. "When Sly sang 'Everyday People' in this wild white space suit I thought Duella would roll over and die right there. What a night! All thanks to my stingy dad." Christian needed someone to listen, to hug him, hold him, and remind him over and over that his father had loved him. When Carlos took his hand as they left the restaurant he leaned into his shoulder and sobbed.

At three a.m., he woke up, mind racing. Carlos was a straight shooter. He had a boyfriend in LA, but they were both careful. The odds of nfection after a single encounter were miniscule. They'd both read lengthy articles documenting the risk of repeated exposures. This deepening tragedy was targeting the sexual outliers the men who were fucking their brains out.

That wasn't them.

Thirty-One

Like countless other gay men, Christian and Carlos fashioned their own Puritan forts, hoping near abstinence would hold the nightmare at bay. But the house of cards they'd carefully constructed collapsed when Carlos called one chilly morning in November.

He talked fast, partially in Spanish, admitting to 'a few relationships in town' in past years. "But I'm not sleeping around. I *swear* to you on that." He'd fallen ill after Isaac's funeral.

"Did you get tested? You know, as a precaution?" Carlos was wailing now, apologizing. "Listen to me Carlos. You need to do that right away," Christian's voice tensed.

"I did," Carlos said, sniveling. "It's positive."

"You need to test again," Christian answered, a sickly cold panic seeping through his veins. "Talk to my cousin at UCS, he's a doctor. We'll take this one step at a time. It could be a false positive. You're young and fit, Carlos. This isn't a death sentence. We'll get through it."

He hung up and slumped into the slipper chair Marge had offloaded from the apartment. He was going to die. When Angie got back from the grocery store, where would he begin? She was always the rational one, taking things in stride, no matter how dark. Ashamed and scared, Christian had turned his charmed life into a nightmare. Now, he wanted it all back desperately. He'd made a dumb roll of the dice, in a moment of grief, and he'd lost.

"So did you use a condom or not?" Angie asked. She'd never questioned Christian's longtime affection for Carlos. She assumed they were smart about it. Why the need to exchange fluids? Some crude tribal ritual? A secret handshake?

"We do, we did … usually," he answered sheepishly. "But I was upset and drunk. We went to dinner and, yes, okay, we had sex. Without a condom. I have no excuses." Angie looked at the love of her life, reduced to a scared middle-aged man. She'd never seen Christian so shaken, shoulders slumped. Her anger flared and, just as quickly, it melted.

"Come over here," she said softly, reaching for him. "Give me a hug. Don't borrow trouble. We'll go see Dr. Cheng in the morning." Christian's small frame crumpled into her arms. His body felt leaner, skin tougher. Hauling brush around the chalet had made him fit. Or was it the smoking? He'd quit after his father died. Angie kissed the top of his head.

"What if I got it?" he asked quietly, tears running out of his eyes. "Angie, I'm petrified."

He knew the symptoms by heart: Night sweats, fevers, weight loss, diarrhea, tongue sores, bruises that didn't heal. None of the above. He'd run through them daily, examining his body inch-by-inch. Asian food was out, Christian told Angie late one afternoon as they contemplated dinner. It hadn't agreed with him lately. The last time they'd ordered Thai, his bowels had been shot for the day.

"Then, it's time," she answered sternly. "There's a doctor in town. Tomorrow morning. We're going. Okay?"

A photograph of Dr. Cheng on Mount Kilimanjaro hung in a cheap frame in his small office in Stowe. He'd moved there from Boston a few years ago. Angie had met him at the grocery store, and they'd fallen into a lively conversation on the benefits of alternative medicine.

Dr. Cheng spoke in a gentle voice. He had an economical manner, neat and precise, with a wise but kind face. "I understand you're concerned about some risky sexual behavior a few months ago," he said, pausing at deliberate intervals, as if he'd studied patient-speak in medical school.

"Yes, once," Christian answered. "But I just found out he is HIV-positive."

"Any fatigue, fever, loss of appetite?" Christian shook his head.

"How about rashes, sore throat, headache, muscle aches? A cold?"

"No."

"Have you noticed swollen lymph nodes?"

"I wasn't checking. But not now."

Christian buttoned his shirt and took the chair next to Angie's. "I want to hear your questions and concerns about the test," Dr. Cheng said, folding his hands across his bony knees.

"I'm not sure I want it today. I don't want results that mean nothing."

"You know, if you contracted this a month ago or more, I'd say your results would be pretty solid. Would I want you to get retested three months from now? Absolutely. Do I need you to promise me you'll avoid behaviors that would put yourself or others at risk? Yes, absolutely."

"Listen: you were exposed, yes," he kept on. "That's not as definitive as it might sound. Let's not fall apart over something that hasn't happened yet. We'll get you tested today. And we'll make an appointment for the results ..." he wheeled himself over to his desk calendar ... "in two weeks from today, the seventeenth."

"Doesn't the first test take only a few days? I want to know if that's positive. I want to know."

Dr. Cheng shook his head. "Can't do that. Any positive result would be preliminary. A positive ELISA gets repeated, then sent out for the Western blot. Lots of reasons you could have a false positive on the ELISA. Syphilis, for one. Drug use. Multiple pregnancies." His delivery was deadpan, but Christian found himself looking up smiling. He could deal with this guy at his sickbed.

"A negative ELISA is pretty damn negative, but I can't tell you I'll call you with that, because then if you *don't* get the call – right? You understand?"

"You think I'd jump off a bridge."

"I can suggest a counselor if you'd like. I'm going to stay right here while Gretchen draws your blood." Christian looked away, the sight of his blood rising into the vial always made him feel weak in the knees. "We have some party favors," Dr. Cheng continued, presenting Christian with an opaque bag of rubbers. "You have five different kinds here. You'll find several of each. Do you know how to use them?" Christian liked Dr. Cheng. His bedside manner was both irreverent and serious. The only way to face this was head-on, try to laugh, wear a condom, and hope for the best.

Dr. Cheng's nurse called to confirm their appointment on the 17th. The results were in, so Christian figured the news wasn't good. He and Angie sat anxiously in the waiting room, flipping through the big *People* expose on Rock Hudson's gay life. When the nurse showed him in, Dr. Cheng's wisecracking was absent. He spoke briskly, though he had to get through something unpleasant.

"I'm sorry to have to tell you that you have HIV." Christian froze, ears began to ring. "But that *doesn't* mean you have AIDS," the doctor continued. "A milder case, like what you have, we call ARC, for AIDS-related complex. I know right now these words sound like gobbledygook. This isn't the news we'd hoped for, but it could be a lot worse. The strain of the virus you have is less virulent."

"Should I make a will?" Christian asked, his voice catching in his throat.

Dr. Cheng looked up at Christian with kind eyes, then over to Angie, who sat quiet but stunned. "Christian, you could have two good years left, maybe more, maybe less. There are people out there living normal, active lives with ARC. The research is moving quickly, but we're racing the clock," he said. "All my patients are. So, yes a will is probably wise. Again, I'm sorry, but we will do everything we can to manage this together."

Christian hadn't grasped the impact of the diagnosis until the words were spoken. He called his father's attorney, hedging a bit, suggesting Isaac's death had inspired him to make a will. Angie would be his beneficiary and executor.

Outwardly, the upbeat clichés about 'beating this thing' buoyed his spirits. But death sentences were difficult to unpack. Would he have a month? A year? Two? He didn't know whether to climb in bed or plan an extravagant trip with Angie. He knew he was dying, but Christian had no idea how to go about it. He was a middle-aged man in otherwise good health.

Thirty-Two

"Now think about the virus as it's seeking cells to attack. Is it angry? In a rush? Sly and devious? Or just plain rude?" Dr. Cheng always brought a fresh way to think about the disease.

"Have you seen that Scrubbing Bubbles commercial on TV?," he asked. "They're soldiers, attacking a toilet bowl. Think of your CD4 cells like that—little Scrubbing Bubbles marching through your body, cleaning up, and getting rid of HIV." Dr. Cheng took to whistling the jingle from the TV commercial.

Christian remained brave, cheerful, and committed, but he wasn't going to kid himself. His time was limited. Promising cures like Bactrim, Pentamidine, HPA-23, Suramin, Foscarnet, and Isoprinosine were being tested in Stockholm, although several doctors discounted their immune boosting potential. "I might as well drink shampoo," Christian quipped. But Isoprinosine was available in Mexico and, already, a pony express system was set up to fetch it from Tijuana. What did it matter? No one knew shit. But everyone was optimistic.

Christian's high fevers and drenching sweats came with greater frequency. Angie changed his pajama top at midnight, again at two a.m., and sometimes again at three-thirty. Although he'd been off of AZT for over a week, his white count was inching up again. He'd be back on it in a few days. Christian previous day's blood tests reported a white count of 800.

But that wasn't possible. It had bottomed out just under 2000 and was on its way up. Christian hadn't started back on AZT, so he wondered how this number had come down. The doctor had no answer. He dumped the disparities on the 'weekend problem,' when the labs are presumably staffed by chimpanzees.

Christian hated this daily monitoring. It served only to remind him that he was dying more rapidly than a week ago. He still looked healthy, but the disease was alive and on the move, despite the positive noise. In April, Dr. Cheng told him his numbers were back in the red zone. He had thrush on his tongue, an ominous sign. In a short time, AIDS had taken over in the same brutal way it had already destroyed 16,000 lives. So much for AIDS-lite.

Angie woke up this morning scared and angry. Her emotions careened between hope and despair. Every day without a cure had exhausted both of them. She could see he was weakening, far less active than last month. Dr. Cheng wasn't optimistic, but he was upbeat. Had the stress of the treatment itself worn him out? Was he deteriorating again? His numbers were unsteady. Angie wasn't sure if she could endure watching him in pain, seeing him suffer as he prepared to die. They had been so focused on new treatments that she hadn't given thought of living without Christian … or considered that he wouldn't last to see a cure.

Christian had become weak and dependent over the past two weeks, so different a few months ago from his days of daily walks in the mountains and talk of recovery, new music, and movies. When she held him at night, praying for his health, she tried to ignore the small purple lesions covering his body, instead trying to transmit her own body's strength, to ward them off. She could see that pain racked his body, even though he was being dosed with 50 milligrams of morphine per hour, up from 30 the prior week. His breathing had become labored and achingly shallow.

"I can feel it," he told her one night. "I'm leaving my body."

"Maybe you are, so let yourself go," she answered. "And I want you to know that as much as I want you here with me, I want you to feel safe and peaceful, more than anything. So if you have to go, it's okay. I love you Christian deGraaf."

"I know death is right around the corner. I've accepted it. I couldn't have gotten this far without you and my mom," he told her. "I'd have given up by now. I watched this with Carlos. The things they say about death, they sound trite. But they are all true. I see the staircase."

At dusk, Christian awoke and struggled to get up out of bed, his face expressionless. Angie, Marge and Dr. Cheng tried to dissuade him. He didn't have the strength to rise, but he insisted. The doctor and three nurses pulled him upright, allowing him to see the shimmery snow and ice outside. "Maybe we should put in a little pond over by the tree line?" he said, pointing out the window. "With our luck, we'd probably hit the sewer line we finally put in a few years ago." After they held him upright, for a moment, Christian allowed himself to be laid back down.

Three hours later, he awoke again and, once more, begged to be allowed to leave his bed. Two of the nurses helped him stand. He was so weak he could not lift his head. Somehow he managed three steps with his arms wrapped around their shoulders before collapsing back on his bed and falling into a deep sleep. His lungs filled with fluids all night. One of the nurses took the chore of putting a tube down his throat to drain them. He lapsed instantly into a coma. His breaths were short, but no longer labored.

"If you can hear me, lift your index finger," she said. Christian did nothing.

She repeated the command, and Christian's finger moved.

Late into the night, Marge and Angie whispered their love into Christian's ears. Long after midnight, one of the nurses asked Christian to move his finger but got no response.

Early the next morning, a sleet storm brought icy pings and plinks to the chalet's windows. The nurse on duty noted his forehead felt cold to the touch, the skin no longer pliable. As the morning progressed, Christian's breathing became irregular. And at 10:20, after a series of brief gasps, his breathing stopped.

Marge and Angie sat with him, talked to him, one last time. Angie told him again how much she loved him and would miss him and what an enormous void he would leave in this world. When Marge returned with the nurses, the color had drained from his face.

At the Church of Heavenly Rest on 90th and Fifth, the 500 mourners entered to the strains of 'Let It Be'. Among them – old agency friends, neighbors, eccentric family members, Duella's people, and a smattering of politicians, musicians, barkeeps, cranks, and city luminaries – all of whom had benefitted from Christian's support, his creativity, and his kindness. One agency friend played a videotape, made just three months ago, of Christian's interview with amfAR. It seemed fitting that he would appear, in living color, at his own funeral.

With his wry humor, he spoke of visions; those who promised to help as he crossed to 'the other side' was able to appear in full-color at his own funeral. People were warmed by Christian's wry humor, warmth and talk of visions of people who promised to help him to 'the other side.'

"How do you describe a star whose too-brief journey lit up so many lives?" Angie asked the mourners. "And now I say to my sweet, dearest friend – go well and be at peace. And as we had so often promised each other, we will always be together, always in love." The church filled with voices singing 'Amazing Grace' and, after the benediction, the mourners filed out to the organist playing "All You Need Is Love," Christian's favorite song.

Thirty-Three

The smell of coffee roused Angie from a deep sleep. Eyes closed in reverie, she inhaled the scent as a cascade of memories washed over her. She felt Christian's presence, sitting on the side of the bed, coaxing her awake gently, holding the cup he'd brewed and poured while making idle mentions of muffins in the oven, crisp bacon, and an omelette on the way. She'd meet his sweet smile, in this way, on so many mornings, his eyes crinkling at the corners in merriment.

"Mmmm, baby …" he'd whisper, taking a bite of bacon as she surfaced to consciousness. Then he'd nuzzle her ear with a salt-cured whisper. "You know you want it …"

She'd worked hard to find happiness alone. But she missed his tender effervescence, the small gestures they'd shared. She ached for his warmth, longed for his wit and mischief. Sometimes at night, as they'd sat alone under the canopy of stars on the deck, Christian would recount the moment he first laid eyes on her. How she took his breath away in Kingston. "Its must have been the headphones," he'd muse. "You were singing as if your whole life depended on it."

"Silly boy," she'd tousle his hair, stroke his cheek. "My whole *rent* depended on it. What would you know of that?" The thought of Carlos made her smile. "Nice move, whisking me off to meet your gay lover. Isn't that what every girl dreams of?" Their story never wore thin. With each retelling, they'd fall into fits of giggles.

Clara had filled the coffee maker, setting the timer before she went to bed. She'd adopted the gesture, inspired by Christian, as a way to thank the renegade aunt who'd become her family, her lifeline, her world. Angie would call her tonight, she thought, as she slipped from under the covers, enticed into the morning to pour herself a cup.

If she hadn't known better, Angie might have guessed a teenaged girls' sleepover had broken out in the living room. The sofa was strewn with pillows and blankets. Paper cups littered the coffee table, along with pretzels, bowls of nuts, and half-empty glasses. How had it happened? A moment of magic, their wild party of three, a lightening strike from the blue. The night had left her feeling lighter, lifted in some way.

Perhaps she wasn't a one-hit wonder after all, Angie thought. The question had galled her for years. Maybe this was the dream she'd deferred? But first, the matter of dinner was ahead. "On it," Clara said. She picked up Italian in town earlier, ready to heat it up.

After dinner, Clara raised her glass in a toast. "You know what we haven't done yet?" she asked, looking over at May, then Angie. "We haven't played the song!" Angie waved them off at first. Goodness gracious, no. Silly girls. But Clara had found the record, and as she turned up the volume on *Deep, Deep, Deep*, it's infectious beat took hold.

Angie rose from the sofa, slowly at first, her inner diva returning. The backbeat spoke to her, stroking a bold spirit, long ago tamed. Feeling the music, she flipped her hair and swivelled her hips, summoning her inner disco diva. *Oooh, how do you like your looooove?* Clara catcalled, and May clapped to the beat, a tipsy audience of two shouting, *"Sing it, Angie!"*

So she did.

Swaying now, Angie traced her fingers up and down her fleece vest, fingering the zipper suggestively. Pausing, teasing, before she yanked it, fast and hard, in a strip tease. Vest overhead, twirling on one finger, Angie delivered Vermont's first burlesque disco show, ripped from the pages of a L.L. Bean catalog.

She was singing in earnest now, a cheese grater standing in for a microphone. *Deep, Deep, Deep … How do you like it? How do you like it?* Against the pulsing backbeat, the ridiculousness of the moment set her free. Each shimmy and shake returned like a long-lost friend. She'd stored these moves in her body, where the choreography had lain dormant, waiting for this moment. Angie rocked, she rolled, she shimmied and two-stepped. With each step, she felt the sex and the shame dissipate; the weight of it all floating away in a vapor, as a feeling of freedom and wholeness was suddenly unleashed.

She'd carried this burden from Lewiston to New York to Lewiston and back to Stowe. Ada had been right, she should live like Holly Golightly. She'd tasted it, but only briefly. When did she plan to live it? The flood of joy and relief might have overwhelmed her, but she had her small audience to consider.

Snapping her fingers, she pointed to Clara who picked up a beer bottle and jumped in to sing backup. *Deep, Deep, Deep* ... they sang the refrain together. Clara had never seen Angie this radient, happy and free. The three of them tipsy-giggled into the wee hours of the morning, riding a wave of release.

May had gotten up early and returned to the Inn to gather her notebooks and cassette tapes, check out, and gas up the rental car for the drive to Manhattan. Now freshly showered, a little worse for wear, she greeted Angie at the door to say goodbye. "How you feeling this morning?"

"I couldn't be happier ... or more relaxed," Angie answered. "A few bottles of wine and a few hours of sleep must have done the trick for me. I suspect I'll require a long nap this afternoon."

May picked up the remaining blankets and folded them neatly into squares, as Clara and Angie gathered up the remaining bowls and glasses for the dishwasher. Once the house was tidy, they moved to the deck, taking in the cool morning air and views of the mountains, sitting together in silence.

When May took her leave, Angie gathered her in a hug. "Thank you, May. You gave me something I didn't know was lost. Now you'll call me when you get home." Angie felt protective. She'd grown fond of May.

"I can't tell you how grateful I am to have met you, Mrs deGraaf. Sorry, *Angie*." They'd come a long way since their awkward beginning on Friday. "I'll leave you to your mountains. Enjoy your peace. I'll be in touch."

As the tires crunched down the gravel driveway, Angie stepped inside and turned up the radio. 'Monday, Monday' was playing. She swayed around the room, while Clara finished packing up her duffle bag and opening the windows to the clear morning.

Angie deGraaf was nobody's prick tease, or victim, rebel aunt or dutiful daughter. She was neither a pop star nor a porn star. A wife, caregiver, now widowed, certainly. But wouldn't Christian want her to find a new song? For the first time in her life, Angie felt whole. She would just allow today to unfold, tomorrow, too. And when she felt ready, Angie deGraaf would do what she'd done so well before.

She would begin, once again.

James Bell

Afterword

The spark for this book came on a beautiful 2022 spring afternoon car ride along the 250 bypass in Charlottesville, Virginia. The dogwoods were out and the town was busy preparing for Historic Garden Week in Virginia and the Dogwood Festival. A NPR fundraising appeal sent me searching for another FM station. A disco downbeat thumped on the radio and a familiar voice began barking out 'More, More, More. How do you like it? How do you like it? More, More, More.' The beat was catchy and it instantly brought back a slew of memories about being eighteen years old again.

A visit to *Wikipedia* brought back 1976 New York City and the story of a disco singer who had a prior career as an adult actress in the early 1970s. Andrea Marie Truden moved to New York from Louisville, Kentucky in late 1960s, appeared in *The Way We Were* and thereafter performed in over 50 adult movies in the early-mid 1970s. Then, as the lead in The Andrea True Connection, she went about making 'More, More, More' a number-one hit forty-six years ago. It still has a familiarity that every teenager of the era instantly remembers, once a few bars of the simple refrain are sung.

I realized an unbelievable New York story was right in front of me if I could sort it all out. New York was, and always is, about 'making it' and that remains the reason why many people move there every day to live. Only in New York can you be a working adult actress, while writing and performing a top-ten pop song that is fondly remembered by a 66-year-old man driving on the 250 bypass, 400 miles from New York. The magic of America.

This fractured fairy tale takes place in New York City between 1965 and 1985. It was a fascinating and volatile period, filled with wonderful characters and striking historical events. While this is a novel, the story is anchored to political, social, athletic and creative individuals who drove the events during the period. In my research and experience, New York has always been -- give or take a mild recession -- America's most dynamic stewpot where people come to achieve their dreams.

The many histories that I read about the city were a joy to lose myself in. The hardest part was trying to select what to include, and who to write about. New York has an endless bounty of stories to pick from. The challenge in writing this book was always where to start.

The book begins with the sunny, but financially reckless optimism of the Lindsay mayoral terms in the 1960s and early 1970s, and ends with a broken, grimy bankrupt city trying to reinvent itself as the global financial center just as 1980s Reaganomics was taking off. The social welfare state was gone and business entrepreneurs had taken over as the new city saviors. Wall Street exploded and New York City moved along with it, adapting, as it always does, to the next era of change.

I read over forty books to better understand this city and time period. Titles ranged from 'Fun City' to 'Fear City', but it was the stories of individuals who made their mark on the city in that period that drew my attention and affection. I moved to New York after most of this story had taken place and worked there for another thirty years, watching New York City mostly prosper through the 1980s and 1990s, becoming the global financial center that withstood September 11, 2001. I was there that day and have watched New York rise again and again with a whole new cast of characters.

New York has always been a decent long-term bet, despite economic ebbs and flows. It will never be dull. My children spent their early working careers in New York too, so it was rewarding to have reasons to regularly visit and watch this next generation settle in and add their stories to the rich lore and history.

It was a blast to create a narrative that accommodated a range of historical interests and memories that dominated my professional life and world view. Re-reading Jimmy Breslin articles made me appreciate even more the voice and the spirit of the era. Like Steve Karmen composed and Milton Glaser designed in 1977, I Love New York and always have, ever since seeing Mary Martin in 'Peter Pan' on Broadway in 1964 with my parents. I hope this story brings the same affection, frustrations, vitality and chuckles to my readers about this wonderful city.

This, like most of my books, was originally a research project that turned into a quasi-novel that is mostly true. In addition to the internet at my fingertips, I read 44 books and hundreds of articles about the city and its people during that period. I felt like a bee in a nudist colony. A perfect place, but where to start?

These books include: James Arena's 'First Ladies of Disco', Harvey Areton's 'When the Garden Was Eden', Ken Auletta's 'The Streets Were Paved With Gold', Steven Blush's 'New York Rock', William Boyd's 'Any Human Heart, Pauline Bren's 'The Barbizon, The New York Hotel That Set Women Free,' Jimmy Breslin's '44', Truman Capote's 'Breakfast at Tiffany's', Jefferson Cowie's 'Staying Alive: The Seventies and the Last Days of the Working Class', Sean Deveney's 'Fun City: John Lindsay, Joe Namath and How Sports saved New York City in the 1960s', Walt Frazier's and Ira Berkow's 'Rockin' Steady,' Josh Friedman's 'Tales of Times Square', Derek Frost's 'Living and Loving in the Age of AIDS,' Wes Gottlock's 'Manhattan's East Village, Three Decades of Madness,' Edward Grazda's 'Mean Streets: NYC 1970-1985, Lawrence Grobel's 'Al Pacino', Bill Gutman's 'Miracle Year 1969: The Amazing Mets and the Super Jets', Debbie Harry's 'Face It: A Memoir', Doug Hill's and Jeff Weingrad's 'Saturday Night: A Backstage History of *Saturday Night Live',* Jack Jones's 'Let Me Take You Down: Inside the Mind of Mark David Chapman', Michelle Kort's 'Soul Picnic: The Music and Passion of Laura Nyro', Bill Landis' 'Sleazoid Express', Mary Wells Lawrence's 'A Big Life', Bill Madden's 'Tom Seaver: A Terrific Life', Jonathan

Mahler's 'The Bronx is Burning: 1977, Baseball, Politics and the Battle for the Soul of the City', Peter Maas's 'Serpico', Rebecca Makkai's 'The Great Believers', Max Millard's '100 New Yorkers of the 1970s',James Andrew Miller's and Tom Shales' 'Live From New York', Legs McNeil's 'The Other Hollywood', Paul Monette's 'Becoming a Man,' 'Borrowed Time: An AIDS Memoir' and 'Last Watch of the Night', Kim Phillips-Fein's 'Fear City: New York's Fiscal Crisis and the Rise of Austerity Politics', Lawrence Scanlon's 'The Horse God Built', Art Shamsky's 'The Magnificent Seasons: How the Jets, Mets and Knicks Made Sports History and Uplifted a City and a Country', Randy Shilts' 'And the Band Played On: Politics, People and the AIDS Epidemic', Bobby Short's and Robert Mackintosh's 'Bobby Short: The Life and Times of a Saloon Singer', Ian Schrager's 'Studio 54', Jean Stein's 'Edie', Sean Strub's 'Body Counts: A Memoir of Activism, Sex and Survival', Alecia Swasy's 'Soap Opera: The Inside Story of Procter & Gamble', Philip Trager's 'New York in the 1970s', Steven Travers' 'The Last Icon. Tom Seaver and His Times', Joseph Viteritti's 'Summer in the City, John Lindsay, New York and the American Dream', George Whitmore's 'Someone Was There', Alice Sedgwick Wohl's 'As It Turns Out: Thinking About Edie and Andy', and Hanya Yanagihara's 'The Paradise.'

This is my eighth novel and first to take on the exciting events that took place over a twenty-five year period in New York City from the mid-1960's to the late 1980's. I spent my entire career working in New York, first in the advertising industry at Ogilvy & Mather, then later in the brand strategy and design world at Lippincott. I was fortunate to be on the team that brought Sugar Bear back as the spokescharacter for Post cereal's Super Golden Crisp in the mid-1980s. I hope that I have rendered the history of the times, events and characters somewhat faithfully, or at least dramatically or comically to life. The rest is where human imagination takes over.

James Bell

Charlottesville, Virginia

Autumn 2024

WILD SIDE

James Bell

Acknowledgments

I want to first thank Heidi, my wife of thirty-eight years for her support and criticism along the way in this attempt to write a bit of New York City fiction and history. She rarely sugar-coated any of her comments and more than once said, 'this is a long, droning mess that needs a lot more work before I will look at it again.'

I also want to thank a small group of friends who provided terrific counsel and active support over the past two years. They include Marvin Bush, David DeCamp, David Foulk, Victoria Horner, Meg Huckaby, Rob Jiranek, Richard Mulligan, Sally Neill, Harry Tower, and Massie Valentine. Their observations and suggestions made this a far better book. In addition, and in particular, I want to thank two individuals: Chip Fortier, a childhood friend, author and editor in Virginia Beach, who helped me shape the initial characters, flow and plot, and Constance Costas, another friend and book editor from Richmond, Virginia, who worked with me to smooth out the narrative and bring the final story to life. And last but certainly not least, I want to thank Barb Wallace for designing the cover for this book, our ninth collaboration! Without all of these good friends, I'd still be tinkering around, going nowhere, lost in the John Lindsay years.

Then there is the unlimited supply of historical information available on line. God bless the internet.

WILD SIDE

James Bell

About the Author

James Bell is an author who lives in Charlottesville, Virginia with his wife of 38 years. Prior to becoming a full time writer, James was a senior executive in the advertising and brand management consulting fields in New York City for over three decades.

His prior seven novels include 'The Screen Door: A Story of Love, Letters & Travel' (2011), 'The Twenty Year Chafe' (2013), 'Christchurch' (2014), 'Crisis in the Congo' (2015), 'American Dreamer' (2019), 'Spook' (2020), and 'Condor' (2022). All of them received effusive praise from a small, yet insightful group of friends and strangers.

WILD SIDE

WILD SIDE

Made in the USA
Columbia, SC
14 April 2025